THE ULTIMATE
GOAL OF GOD

THE ULTIMATE
GOAL OF GOD

A Wonderful Journey
from Logic to Love

Wade Travis

WESTBOW
PRESS
A DIVISION OF THOMAS NELSON

WestBow Press books may be ordered through booksellers or by contacting:

WestBow Press
A Division of Thomas Nelson
1663 Liberty Drive
Bloomington, IN 47403
www.westbowpress.com
1-(866) 928-1240

ISBN: 978-1-4497-1492-5 (sc)
ISBN: 978-1-4497-1493-2 (dj)
ISBN: 978-1-4497-1491-8 (e)

Library of Congress Control Number: 2011926920

Printed in the United States of America

WestBow Press rev. date: 4/14/2011

Contents

Preface

Commissioned to teach at a local church, I turned to God each Monday to seek counsel of what it was that he wanted me to teach the following Sunday. Believing in the answers that came to me, I would then research, type and teach. But approximately ten months later, as I looked back toward the beginning of the class and all that had been taught, I noticed something amazing. God had given us an introduction followed by key healing points and I was about to teach a wonderful and dramatic conclusion. I immediately felt the need to get this information to a larger audience and began to think about a book. But it wasn't until the simple comment "You need to write a book" was repeated to me several times that I finally took notice, retrieved all materials taught, a note pad, a pen and began praying for God's guidance and wisdom. Once again the final results became more astonishing than anything I had ever imagined.

The intent of this book is to give you the most powerful truth in as few words as possible so that you can concentrate on its strength and its purpose. It will direct you from an introduction of logic and guide you to God's loving arms as you learn and then achieve the ultimate goal of God.

Acknowledgments

Of course credit for this book belongs to God, but it is with great pleasure that I also recognize and give thanks to Terry Benner, Lyle Travis, Wade Estes, Ken Cross, Terry Holiday, Wayne Sparks and Gary Kuhlman. These people placed themselves as obedient to God and would thereby serve as God had intended to become men of great influence as they gave of their time and patience. It is such devoted men and women across the world that God uses to touch the lives and hearts of many others so that they too may know the love God has for all.

1

Is There a God?

One would think that in a book titled *The Ultimate Goal of God*, the reader would already believe in God and therefore God would be assumed, but I strongly believe that this is the first topic we need to address because of the complacencies of our Christian faith. And that's just it, "Faith". We are told that we need to have faith, or take it in faith. But it's incomprehension of true faith that affords us the ability to live our lives just sort of taking God in faith, or for granted, when in fact we are not truly living in undisputable belief. We therefore have doubts and find ourselves at times wondering if there truly is a God. So let us address this.

Is there a God?

In today's society we seem to have a great many people that believe in the concept of a God. Some believe because they feel something tugging at their hearts. Still others believe because they merely want something to believe in. And then there are those that simply believe because they were brought up in a Christian family. They have known no other way of life. It's what they grew up with. Never question, never doubt. If the doubts should come up they simply toss them out of their minds for fear of sacrilege. This chapter is here to address this and bring forth an **absolute proof** that God is real.

Pastor Mike Moran once stated in front of his congregation that when you read the Bible you should "wrestle with the scriptures." I couldn't agree more. In fact you should wrestle with your belief of God as well. Let me explain. When you read the Bible looking for answers and are trying to understand, wrestle with it until you no longer see it from man's point of view and start seeing it from God's point of view. You have to be willing to question the scriptures until the Holy Spirit (our counselor) helps you understand what God is revealing. The same goes with your belief in God. You need to wrestle with it until the Counselor gives you absolute proof.

For those of you who feel something tugging at your heart, you are not wrong. First of all there is evidence in your surroundings. Paul states in Romans 1:20

> *For since the creation of the world God's invisible qualities - his eternal power and divine nature - have been clearly seen, being understood from what has been made, so that men are without excuse.*

David points out in Psalm 19:1-4

> *The heavens declare the glory of God;*
> *   the skies proclaim the work of his hands.*
> *Day after day they pour forth speech;*
> *   night after night they display knowledge.*
> *There is no speech or language*
> *   where their voice is not heard.*
> *Their voice goes out into all the earth,*
> *   their words to the ends of the world.*

There is evidence every day that proves we have a God amongst us. But Satan puts up a very good smoke screen, or fog, causing people not to see the very things that are around them. It is said that "if Satan can't make you bad, he'll make you busy. If he can make you busy long enough, he can make you bad", meaning that he can then keep your eyes off of the very evident surroundings that would prove to you that God is in fact in every created thing. But most people believe that there is some kind of God, because God is not trying to keep himself hidden from us. As David and Paul point out, God makes himself obvious in the creations around us, but he will also make himself obvious (that means beyond the shadow of doubt) to our hearts if we will only seek to know him.

So now I would like to un-complicate and contemplate some very simple concepts that need to be addressed, sort of getting back to the basics. Let us first address what is a God. We will tackle who he is later.

According to the dictionary it states that a God is:

1. The Supreme Being; The eternal and infinite Spirit.
2. Creator and Sovereign of the universe.
3. Divine, Supreme, Infinite Mind, Spirit, Soul, Principle, Life, Truth, Love.

This is obviously man's attempt to describe what a God is. But as we said, let's get back to basics. So by using pure common sense I believe we will achieve a better understanding of what a God is. We can simplify it in two key points.

Key Point One
God would be all creating.

If we truly comprehend the concept of a God, it has to be understood that a God would have complete understanding, complete knowledge, complete power and complete divinity. Complete ability to do all things. That would be a true understanding of a God. This means a God would have the ability to be a creator. And being a creator this God would have the power to create all things, not just some things, because that would not be the mark of a true God, or true creator. A true God would not just have power to create the sun but not the moon, the ground but not the ocean, or the crops but not the rain.

The "Common Sense Concept" of a God means that a God would have to have all power, all knowledge and all creativity.

Understand this: If a God truly has this kind of power then a God would not need the help of any other gods. In fact there could not even be any other gods. **This comprehension becomes the very undisputable proof that there can only be one God, or one Creator.**

Key Point Two
God would be all loving.

If God is a true and complete creator then God would have an absolute love for the creation. Not a worldly understanding of love but an absolute love. This creating God would thereby wish to protect, care for and cherish the creation. If the creation should become endangered, the true creator would take the steps necessary to protect the creation.

Let me put it to you this way: If you as a mother or father should find your own son or daughter had slipped off a cliff and was now hanging on a ledge crying out for help, would you not put your own life in danger to find a way to bring that child to safety? Now if you as a mere parent would do this for a child that you bore, would not the love of a creator do as much? The fact is the absolute love that a creator would have for the creation would compel the creator to do even more to save the life of that creation. Therefore a true God would have to do whatever is necessary to protect the life of that creation because of the absolute love a true creator would have.

This comprehension becomes the proof of what the heart and actions of a true God, or true Creator, would display.

In contrast, the heart and actions of one that could not create would be just the opposite. A non-creator would have jealousy and hatred for the creation because he does not have the ability to create.

In John 10:10a it states:

The thief comes only to steal and kill and destroy.

This scripture reveals that Satan does not have the ability to create, because he has no absolute love for the creation, and in fact wants to destroy it. Thus, Satan cannot be a real God.

Let us recap for a moment:

1. A true God would be all creating and all loving.
2. A false god would not have the ability to create and would indeed hate the creation and want it destroyed.

With this knowledge let us now expose the different theologies of past and present to the "Common Sense Concept" to reveal which actions and hearts are conducive to that of a real God.

As we study ancient history we find many times that someone or something is titled god.

1. The Canaanite's god Baal was a god of the elements who brought rain and made the ground fruitful. They were led to

believe that this god would be pleased if they would cut their arms to show their loyalty.

2. The Phoenicians and Canaanites had a god called Asherah, the goddess of fertility. They would then partake in sexual rituals to appease this goddess.

3. The Ammonites had a god called Moloch. They believed this god to be a protecting god, and that sacrificing their own children by placing the child on the heated outstretched arms of the statue (burning them alive) would appease this god.

4. Egypt at one time had many gods. There were more than 2000 gods represented in the Egyptian Pantheon. There were gods of the sun, moon, rain, etc. Even the pharaohs themselves (mere men) were believed to be able to achieve god-hood.

5. The Romans also believed in a multitude of gods, including a god for grain, a god for music, and even a protectress of fertility, just to name a few.

In these ancient beliefs we see teachings of both multi-gods and of gods that would have you kill the innocent, such as a child, or hurt yourself to show loyalty to that god. When we compare the "Common Sense Concept" with these ancient theologies we expose them as non-creators for the following reasons:

If it is a god with limited power (the ability to only create one or two things) then it could not be a true God.

If it is a god that asks you to cut or harm yourself to prove your loyalty to it, then it could not be a true God because a God with absolute love would not want you to harm yourself in any way.

If it is a god that asks you to kill the innocent (such as a child) then again it does not have absolute love for the creation and could not be a true God.

This exposure reveals that none of these before-mentioned gods could possibly be a true God and in fact could only be Satan trying to destroy the creation. They have not the love of a creator or the ability to create.

As we ponder the obvious misguiding of these ancient religions it is easy to find ourselves shaking our heads in disbelief that people would succumb to such a belief, but before you allow yourself to judge remember that these people were raised into their beliefs (as were many of us) and let us not forget that today we still see people pick up the paper to read their horoscope.

As we study and compare the ancient religions of yesterday with today, we see a lot of similarities. There is still a belief that a mere human can achieve god-hood, key word "achieve", and this temptation goes all the way back to Adam and Eve. There is still a belief, and we have seen examples in the news and in recent history books within the last hundred years, of a god that wants people to kill the innocent in order to achieve a superior race or superior religion. There is even still a religion that believes in the sacrifice of one's own child. All of this is happening all around us in modern day.

Again none of these can show the absolute love of a God. And let me make this clear. The belief that a human can achieve god-hood means that no God could exist at all. Common sense tells us that the idea that a man can become a God means that we are all equal and we would not need a God, nor could a God exist because there would be no need for a creator. This belief erases the whole understanding of what a true God is.

We can go on with many different religions and beliefs and fill page after page but I believe, using the "Common Sense Concept", you can reveal or expose any and every religion that is brought to your attention. We now have the tools that will bring us true knowledge to show us which God is real and which ones are not. So let us now get to the point of this chapter.

Who is God and do we have absolute proof?

History books tell us of events that happened that will explain different theologies. The Bible tells us of different theological events that will explain history.

Every time an archeological find is made we see more and more proof that the Bible definitely correlates with different historical facts, but the Bible is not a history book. The Bible is documentations of the coexistence of God and man. In the Old Testament it writes of a God that set up a nation to teach the rest of the world that there is only one God, who he is and that he is on his way. The New Testament writes of a man named Jesus as the fulfillment of the Old Testament.

It's important at this time to express that this Jesus is not just mentioned in the New Testament, he is also mentioned in the history books. The history books tell us that Jesus was a compassionate man who led a small group of men around the nation teaching love, healing the sick and giving sight to the blind.

The New Testament indeed states that Jesus led a small group of men around the nation teaching love, healing the sick and giving sight to the blind, but remember the Bible is documentations of the coexistence of God and man, so it also explains why he did these things and that he also raised people from the dead. In three different occasions the Bible tells of Jesus raising people to life once again while a disbelieving crowd either mocked him or watched in confusion.

In the first event Jesus and his disciples are simply approaching a new town when they come upon a funeral possession for a widow's only son.

Luke 7:12-15

As he approached the town gate, a dead person was being carried out-the only son of his mother, and she was a widow. And a large crowd from the town was with her. When the lord saw her, his heart went out to her and he said, "Don't cry." Then he went up and touched the coffin, and those carrying it stood still. He said, "Young man, I say to you, get up!" The dead man sat up and began to talk, and Jesus gave him back to his mother.

The second event is of a little girl who was sick when it was brought to Jesus' attention. As he was on his way to heal the child, and kept busy by a crowd and the healing of a woman's affliction, the little girl died.

Luke 8:49-55

While Jesus was still speaking, someone came from the house of Jairus, the synagogue ruler. "Your daughter is dead," he said. "Don't bother the teacher any more." Hearing this, Jesus said to Jairus, "Don't be afraid; just believe, and she will be healed." When he arrived at the

> *house of Jairus, he did not let anyone go in with him except Peter, John and James, and the child's father and mother. Meanwhile, all the people were wailing and mourning for her. "Stop wailing," Jesus said. "She is not dead but asleep." They laughed at him, knowing that she was dead. But he took her by the hand and said, "My child, get up!" Her spirit returned, and at once she stood up. Then Jesus told them to give her something to eat.*

On the third event the Bible tells us that Jesus this time makes the situation public to demonstrate his authority over death given him by the Father.

John 11:38-44

> *Jesus, once more deeply moved, came to the tomb. It was a cave with a stone laid across the entrance. "Take away the stone," he said. "But, Lord," said Martha, the sister of the dead man, "by this time there is a bad odor, for he has been there four days." Then Jesus said, "Did I not tell you that if you believed, you would see the glory of God?" So they took away the stone. Then Jesus looked up and said, "Father, I thank you that you have heard me. I knew that you always hear me, but I said this for the benefit of the people standing here, that they may believe that you sent me." When he had said this, Jesus called in a loud voice, "Lazarus, come out!" The dead man came out, his hands and feet wrapped with strips of linen, and a cloth around his face. Jesus said to them, "Take off the grave clothes and let him go."*

These New Testament writings state that this Jesus had power over death but then we later read that he never stopped the Romans from crucifying him. Why? Was he just another man and therefore did not have the power over death that the Bible teaches? If so, when he died did that disperse his followers and his teachings? According to an understanding of the New Testament the answer is no! We are still reading of his teachings over two thousand years later because the followers of Jesus reported and documented that Jesus, who was proven to indeed be dead, literally came back to life, walked and talked among several eye-witness accounts which are also recorded in the historical writings of Josephus, and then rose up right in front of them to ascend to heaven.

Strength is given to the New Testament because as we contemplate the writings of the men that had followed and learned from this Jesus, we see that they literally went to their death to proclaim what they were saying and writing was truth.

It is important to understand that most men would not knowingly choose to die or be tortured to death just to preserve a lie that he himself created, much less to get several men to express the same thing and stand firm unto their deaths. **This could only mean that it was truth they discovered and could not dispute.**

So, this brings us back to the before-mentioned question about Jesus. If he had the power to raise people from the dead then why would he let the Romans beat, whip, torture and crucify him unto death?

Was it to show that he was God and had power to stand up against man? If that was the case he could have just spoken a word and the creation would have been destroyed. But according to what these men wrote and took to their death, Jesus was God.

It states in John 1:1-4

> *In the beginning was the Word, and the Word was with God, and the Word was God. He was with God in the beginning. Through him all things were made; without him nothing was made that has been made. In him was life, and that life was the light of men.*

So if what these followers said about Jesus is true (that he is God) then there must have been some other significant reason for him to let the Romans kill him.

In order to understand the reason we must first step back to the Old Testament teachings. We are told in the Old Testament that God created Adam and Eve (the first man and woman) and placed them in a garden called the Garden of Eden where man had need for nothing. It was simply a miraculous place for man to live amongst God. But the story also tells us that man turned his back on God.

Understand that it is "Natural Law" that if a creation should ever decide that it did not need its creator and walked away, it would die. We could compare it with the body saying it doesn't need the very air that it breathes, which we know gives it life. The creation cannot exist without the help of its creator because without the creator there would not even be the earth on which to stand or the air to breathe.

So there it is. In the Old Testament we see that the creation, because of its own choice, will die. If what the creation did by choosing itself over God is considered sin then it is condemned by its own selfish actions to die. We then become a creation without hope. But the creator would not want the creation to die because it has an absolute love for the creation. A true God or true creator would thereby take the steps necessary to save the life of his creation.

So what could possibly be done to preserve the life of a condemned and sinful creation? There is but one solution: If a perfect life (or one that is without sin) were to give up his life to pay for that sin, and being perfect it would thereby pay for all sins. Understand that one who is perfect is better than all that have sinned, for one who is perfect is worth more than all that have sinned. But who is perfect other than God? Answer: no one! So God out of absolute love, in order to save his creation, would be compelled to sacrifice himself so that the creation would not die.

In the book of John we read that as Jesus was conversing with Nicodemus, a member of the Jewish council, he reveals God's absolute love and his intentions in John 3:16

> *For God so Loved the world, that he gave his only begotten Son, that whosoever believeth in him should not perish, but have everlasting life.* KJV

This teaches us that Jesus had a higher purpose to his life and that he knew what that purpose was, which was to give up his life so that all sins would be paid for. Jesus even shows us that he alone is able to give up his life for all sins when he asks a very bold question that no one but God himself could ask without being mocked.

John 8:46

> *Can any of you prove me guilty of sin? If I am telling the truth, why don't you believe me?*

Jesus continues to show his validity while speaking in the temple area. John 10:30

> *I and the Father are one.*

Also in John 10:38c

> *The Father is in me, and I in the Father.*

And in John 14:6 it is written:

I am the way and the truth and the life. No one comes to the Father except through me. If you really knew me, you would know my Father as well. From now on, you do know him and have seen him.

Jesus also shows his authority over death in John 10:17

The reason my Father loves me is that I lay down my life - only to take it up again. No one takes it from me, but I lay it down of my own accord. I have authority to lay it down and authority to take it up again.

With all the before mentioned scriptures it is understood that the different writers were saying that Jesus is God. According to these writings Jesus showed that he had power over death but then went on to allow the Romans to crucify him, which then pays for all sins and thereby gives life back to the creation. He then showed that he had the power to raise himself from the dead to give proof to his sacrifice and further the understanding of his power, authority and God's love for the creation and thereby help us to understand to this day God's grace and mercy. So I ask you, is that not absolute love?

As we use the "Common Sense Concept" on the teachings of the New Testament we can see that we do indeed have proof that a God does exist because of the love shown to protect and save the life of the condemned creation. For the life and teachings of Jesus show that he taught with authority, was compassionate, had power to heal, gave sight to the blind, drove out demons, gave life back to those that had died and, most importantly, gave up his own sinless life and raised it back again to pay for all sins of a condemned creation. This shows us that he indeed had the absolute love of that of a true creator for the creation.

Herein lies the absolute proof that there is a God and that he is Jesus.

This kind of compassion and love proves that Jesus is God.

2

Understanding Grace

The "Common Sense Concept" comprehension taught in the first chapter gives the absolute proof that thoroughly stabilizes Jesus as God. This gives the Bible credibility and allows us to use it for reference. It is now important to understand exactly what God did for us by placing himself on the Cross. In order to do this we must first research and understand grace, more importantly God's grace, which we will address later.

So what is grace?

In the dictionary it states that grace is:

a. Favor shown in granting a delay or temporary immunity.

b. A manifestation of favor, especially by a superior.

c. Unmerited favor.

d. Clemency; pardon; mercy.

In order to fully grasp the strength of these words depicting grace we need to first step back to an understanding of ancient kings and the method of leadership deployed in order to keep full control of their kingship. This will help us to understand grace from man's point of view and later compare it with grace from God's point of view.

Man, being fallible and mortal, had to take great measures to uphold his kingdom or leadership. He would be vulnerable to attacks, poisons or ploys that could uproot him from his high place. A king's leadership must not be trifled with or the protection of his territories or providences would be compromised.

If someone or some group of people should challenge his authority, once they were captured they would be dealt with severely to administer fear in the minds of the people. If absolute rule was not established it would allow rebellion and complete chaos over the land and would thereby expose their territory to other expanding kingdoms. Therefore a king would deploy laws that would command respect as well as give him certain protections. For example, he would only allow his most loyal subjects to come near his domain. He would have someone to watch over his food and would employ a cupbearer to manage his wine. In the book of Nehemiah of the Old Testament Nehemiah clearly states his position as an officer to the king.

Nehemiah 1:11c

I was cupbearer to the king.

Cupbearers were high ranking officers within the royal courts. They had to be completely trusted and respected to hold such a position. They would watch over the wine to guard it from poison and would be expected on occasions to drink the wine before serving it. If poison was administered the cupbearer's death would expose it. A cupbearer is expendable, a king is not.

Although Nehemiah was a trusted and respected official to the king he still had to follow a very strict protocol as we see in Nehemiah 2:1, 2

In the month of Nisan in the twentieth year of King Artaxerxes, when wine was brought for him, I took the wine and gave it to the king. I had not been sad in his presence before; so the king asked me, "Why does your face look so sad when you are not ill? This can be nothing but sadness of heart." I was very much afraid.

Nehemiah went on to speak to the king expressing his concerns but we can comprehend the danger of even an official that could be put to death just for looking sad in the presence of the king.

Other rules employed would not allow you to address the king unless the king acknowledged you first. No one could approach a king for fear of losing their life unless he was first summoned, and in some instances we hear that they were required to come in with their head down and not look into the eyes of the king while they spoke.

When a law or decree was given by a king it was absolute. Once it was sealed by the king's ring it became a proclamation and you would be expected to carry out that proclamation or the penalty would be death. We see an example of this in the Old Testament in Daniel 6:15, 16

> *Then the men went as a group to the king and said to him, "Remember, O king, that according to the law of the Medes and Persians no decree or edict that the king issues can be changed." So the king gave the order, and they brought Daniel and threw him into the lions' den. The king said to Daniel, "May your God, whom you serve continually, rescue you!"*

While enforcing laws to strengthen kingships we see that commoners and even certain officials could get caught up in law which could become their demise. We even see where officials could ensnare someone by using law to eliminate a foe as in the example of Daniel above. Because of a proclamation decreed by this king, Daniel had broken the law just by praying to his God. Daniel was forced to make a decision whether to obey the king and only pray to him, which would save his life, or continue to pray to his God. We read that he chose to obey his beliefs and in this case God spared his life by closing the mouths of the lions.

In the book of Esther we read that even the king's wife was held to strict rules and would be in fear for her life should she ever disrespect certain protocol. Mordecai (Esther's cousin) was trying to convince Esther to approach the king in order to save his people when Esther replied:

> *"All the king's officials and the people of the royal provinces know that for any man or woman who approaches the king in the inner court without being summoned the king has but one law: that he be put to death. The only exception to this is for the king to extend the gold scepter to him and spare his life."* Esther 4:11

In the case of Daniel it is evident that not even the king could rescue someone once the proclamation was in place, but we read in some circumstances how kings did have certain powers in which they could spare or pardon particulars as in the case of Esther 5:1-3

On the third day Esther put on her royal robes and stood in the inner court of the palace, in front of the king's hall. The king was sitting on his royal throne in the hall, facing the entrance. When he saw Queen Esther standing in the court, he was pleased with her and held out to her the gold scepter that was in his hand. So Esther approached and touched the tip of the scepter. Then the king asked, "What is it, Queen Esther? What is your request?"

This king by extending the scepter was able to save the queen's life and thereby becomes an example of human grace which as stated before is "a manifestation of favor by a superior, or an unmerited favor".

We can understand they had to be strict in order to preserve their way of life. In the case of Esther we can understand why the king would grant a pardon because of the innocence of the person caught up in the law. But what if the person was guilty? For example, a person stole something and the penalty was the cutting off of the offending hand. The person stealing knew it was wrong and that it would not be tolerated. They, knowing the law, would thereby have no excuse. If caught they could only stand in front of the king beset with their shame while waiting for their sentence. Now if the king granted them a pardon and did something like put them to work in his garden which would thereby help to maintain his kingdom (assuming they were not a fool) would they not be in debt to him? Would this not set a desire to never disobey that king again and would they not become a model citizen?

Man's grace would be of one person with the ability to pardon, granting immunity to another person of an offence, thus allowing that person to be free from a known punishment or a pending doom, or in this case the saving of an offender's hand. But in this chapter we wish to comprehend God's grace and what he did by placing himself on the cross, so let us compare the ancient kings with God.

First of all God is not dependent upon us so he does not need to pardon or give grace to anybody to maintain his kingdom. He could simply place everything in order so that it maintained itself.

Second, the laws would be different.

1. Kings have judicial laws.
2. God has spiritual laws.

A king is more concerned with judicial laws to protect him from being overthrown or killed. God, of course, is not susceptible to death so he does not need to have judicial law in order to keep his command. God, being perfect, has spiritual laws that are naturally in place which is why he cannot have sin, nor could he allow sin to be with him in heaven. Sin is anything other than Godly principle.

When we read Genesis in the Old Testament we learn God created mankind to enjoy, cherish and love. He intended us to live forever with him and gave us a body accordingly and free will.

Question: If God knew we had the potential to choose sin, why would he give us free will?

Simple… he wanted us to experience what it is to love so he gave us a soul to think and be an individual. He made each and every one of us unique for a purpose. The love we can experience will help us to know God and what he is all about, and as we learn about God we can use this free will to love him for who he is.

In Genesis we learn that when Satan tempted free will it caused mankind to sin by choosing for himself, which is selfishness. Man inadvertently chose to live without God, for selfishness is sin and spiritual law cannot permit sin to be in the presence of God. Not if the true comprehension of a God is to be maintained. It's important to note that sin means "missing the mark". Man is clearly missing the mark and his sin caused him to step out of the protection provided by God. A creation cannot survive without the help of its creator and since the creation literally chose itself before God, natural law tells us that the creation is condemned because it cannot become independent of itself and therefore is doomed to die. It's as if mankind told God that it doesn't need him and in fact that is basically what we did.

Romans 3:23

For all have sinned, and fall short of the glory of God.

We therefore become a "Creation without Hope" as stated in the previous chapter.

After the sin God placed us in a new environment and our bodies became subject to physical law which produces physical death. Understand that when man chose himself over God he became like a fish that felt he was free enough to leave the water. A fish is not free to leave the water; in fact we know that it will die. Man without God is subject to physical laws. A man cannot live without God any more than the fish could live without the water, so when man decided to sin, because of spiritual law, he literally stepped away from God and his protection and thus he became subject to die a physical death. So it is said that the penalty of sin is death.

But what about the soul?

When we look at life from a worldly comprehension we see life with a beginning and an end. We are born and later we die. But that is only what we see. Remember God created us to live forever and forever our souls shall live. We are subject to natural law because of sin and after we die to this body our soul will move on to another place which is called hell. Hell is a place that has total lack of God, or total selfishness. There is not one shred of love or existence of God. It is a place of absolute abandonment, selfishness, torment and suffering. So, we are doomed to live forever without God. We chose selfishness and selfishness we shall have. So here we are living in bodies that naturally decay in a world filled with love and selfishness trying to make order out of complete chaos. Sin has twisted life beyond the comprehension of the simplicity of truth.

As stated in chapter one, God, being a true creator and having the absolute love of a creator, would not wish for his creation to live forever without him because he knows what that would entail. He knows the torment that goes without love, more importantly without God's love.

So what could be done to save a creation that chose to live for itself without God?

Answer: for God to forgive that sin. Ah, but the sinful act brought on the penalty of death and therefore so it demands.

The Apostle Paul stated it well in Romans 6:23 when he wrote:

"For the wages of sin is death, but the gift of God is eternal life in Christ Jesus our Lord."

Jesus took the form of man and lived a sinless life so that he could offer up forgiveness and mercy to his adored creation.

John 1:1, 2

In the beginning was the Word, and the Word was with God, and the Word was God. He was with God in the beginning.

John 1:10

He was in the world, and though the world was made through him, the world did not recognize him.

John 1:14a

The Word became flesh and made his dwelling among us.

After showing himself to be God and living a sinless life, Jesus, by letting the Romans crucify him, became death and gave us the freedom to choose love over selfishness and the ability to say "I'm sorry God. Please forgive me." He literally handed himself over to Satan (the enemy) so that he could pay the price that mankind was to bear. He gave eternal life back to us through his grace and erased all sin by his shed blood and cleansing mercy. We no longer are a creation without hope.

Isaiah 43:25

I, even I, am he who blots out
your transgressions, for my own sake,
and remembers your sins no more."

Pastor Terry Benner (a very wise man), in order to help the understanding and the importance of Jesus, stated "Jesus came to make Satan less important. Jesus came to make sin less important." No truer words could be spoken for it is only because of Jesus and his grace that our lives are spared.

John 6:47

I tell you the truth, he who believes has everlasting life.

Romans 8:1

Therefore, there is now no condemnation for those who are in Christ Jesus, because through Christ Jesus the law of the Spirit of life set me free from the law of sin and death.

Ancient kings could only offer up man's grace preserving our present life but God's grace offers up eternal life and a new body without decay or age. By believing in what Jesus did and asking God for forgiveness we are not only pardoned of our sins but eternal life with God and his everlasting love is promised. This becomes the true understanding of God's grace.

John 1:14b

> *We have seen his glory, the glory of the One and Only, who came from the Father, full of grace and truth.*

3

Diluting the Deity

King David and Paul wrote about the miraculous findings and divine expressions of the creations of this world and how God made himself prevalent and obvious in all things. As Paul states, this provides mankind with no excuse because God has shown himself to all things, but it leaves us short of understanding the salvation offered to us. It is therefore up to man to teach others of the love and salvation of God. Of course Satan does not wish for man to spread the word so he works in many ways to make less the importance and strength of the knowledge of God, sort of "Diluting the Deity".

In Old Testament times they recognized God as the creator of all things great and small, so they followed and worshiped with a fear that God, being magnificent, would have the power to crush and destroy any known foe or evil. They also believed that God would reward those that were good but would cause toils and troubles for any that would oppose, which is why we read in the book of Job that his friend's assumed fault was his believing God would not punish the good. They believed that if mere man should ever cross God, God could just destroy him much like man steps on an ant. Therefore a natural respect was born in every mind and heart that would come to believe in God.

The New Testament teaches of how the love of God reaches far beyond the understanding of man by sacrificing himself in order to give life back to repented hearts. One would think that this miraculous story about Jesus and what a wonderful act of love it tells would be so overwhelming to our everyday common sense that nothing could ever dispute the fact and truth, causing mankind to run to churches, drop to their knees and pray for such an everlasting gift. But this is not the case, for mankind has to struggle to help others to see through a fog of diminishing lies before they realize the gift before them.

It's interesting to note New Testament scriptures that show evidence of fear that the evil spirits have of God, whereas mankind continues to live without the slightest fear of God and his awesome power. Why?

Matthew 8:28, 29

When [Jesus] arrived at the other side in the region of the Gadarenes, two demon-possessed men coming from the tombs met him. They were so violent that no one could pass that way. "What do you want with us, Son of God?" they shouted. "Have you come here to torture us before the appointed time?"

Mark tells of a similar account of another man filled with an evil spirit in Mark 1:24

"What do you want with us, Jesus of Nazareth? Have you come to destroy us? I know who you are - the Holy One of God!"

The evil spirits expressed in these two accounts admit their fear and lack of strength against Jesus, whereas Jesus, while scolding the Pharisees who refuse to comprehend the very scriptures they profess to live by, exposes Satan as the father of all lies.

John 8:43, 44

Why is my language not clear to you? Because you are unable to hear what I say. You belong to your father, the devil, and you want to carry out your father's desire. He was a murderer from the beginning, not holding to the truth, for there is no truth in him. When he lies, he speaks his native language, for he is a liar and the father of lies.

This tells us that Satan is a liar and will use any un-truth necessary to destroy or distort the relationship between God and mankind.

In chapter one we pointed out that God is a God of love. In chapter two we discussed why God gave us free will. These two beautiful opportunities and attributes of God that were meant to enhance our lives are the very things that Satan has used against us to create in us our own individual world where we have come to be more important.

God, creating us for a relationship with him, gives us every opportunity to repent and turn our hearts away from sinful nature and back to him, so God's love is slow to anger. King David understood this when he wrote Psalm 30:4, 5b

Sing to the Lord, you saints of his;
praise his holy name.
For his anger lasts only a moment,
but his favor lasts a lifetime.

We therefore will not always see an immediate consequence to our actions which Satan uses to dilute fear, and with no fear, if we come to believe a need is more satisfying than the long term consequence, we will disobey and sin against God to better care for our lives. **In our selfish moment we unknowingly take advantage of God's love**.

When God gave us free will it was to help us grasp an understanding of real love and the beautiful life it has to offer. When used properly it gives us a greater respect, greater comprehension and greater love for God. It was meant to be beautiful but because free will has selfish tendencies Satan will tempt it and use it to our disadvantage.

Understand that when free will is not used to reach for the true life that God had intended but for selfish gain, then the very nature of free will to give life becomes sin and therefore takes life away, for the wages of sin is death.

So how could Satan diminish such a respect and reverence of God?

Answer: **Time, Accusations and Influence**

Used cleverly, Satan can use these tools to take away understanding, erase feelings of love, diminish the strength of truth or separate mankind from his God.

Time

In very early scriptures we see that Satan began using time as a factor to bring distance between God and creation. In the story of Adam and Eve we learn of the temptation and sin of mankind and how they were put out of the Garden of Eden to toil and work the land. As families expanded and moved to different lands it became the obligation of each to share with their children and their children's children an understanding of God.

Deuteronomy 4:9

Only be careful, and watch yourselves closely so that you do not forget the things your eyes have seen or let them slip from your hearts as long as you live. Teach them to your children and to their children after them.

However, some of the generations were not taught, so whole families, lands and kingdoms knew not of any God nor of the relationship he created us for. This led to a moral decay of ideas and hearts, thus allowing selfish tendencies to abound in such a manner that mankind has become depraved. Also as time progressed we naturally became a world filled with people that have come to know God and people that don't believe at all.

Another tactic of time that Satan used and still uses is with families that did pass on knowledge to their children but did not seek to know God. As future generations, who had been told there was a God, sought to know God, then Satan gave them one. He knows that if man wants to believe in a God then it is better to misdirect them to a false god than to let them follow the real one. And then he will cause them to blindly believe with such strength that they never even research the contradictions of the very stories of that god. He will surround them with such lies that they can no longer see any truth at all. And, as with Adam and Eve, Satan will even push the idea that mankind can become a god, or like god. Throughout history we see examples and beliefs as Satan provides for the selfish desires of our free will to be one that everybody else serves, or the one that everybody else bows down to. This too is another false god, for mankind can no more be God any more than he can live without the air that God created for us to breathe.

In the book of Job we read that God, after Job questions an understanding of God's actions, calmly redirects Job's attitude and understanding of what is man's strength as compared with God in one powerful question.

Job 38:4a

Where were you when I laid the earth's foundation?

Man never had and never will have power of his own accord to create an earth, heavens and solar system. He is dependent solely upon God and what God allows.

Individual time is probably the most powerful tactic of Satan in his quest to keep mankind from the comprehension of God. If a person who knows not of God should keep themselves busy with life and time schedules then they are more apt to overlook God. If a person strives to accomplish then Satan will try to keep them from being content which will have them ever moving, ever tasking and therefore never searching for God. Worse yet, if this person should become self-sufficient and successful then they will feel they have no need for any God at all. If the subject of God should come up, Satan would have them believe that man created God instead of God creating man. They will go on to live life in fullness only to realize when this body passes and they move on to the next life that they have made the wrong decisions.

Mark 8:36

What good is it for a man to gain the whole world, yet forfeit his soul?

Every one of these time topics discussed so far is used by Satan to keep an intermix of non-believers coupled amongst believers to create a world where selfish tendencies are not only tolerated but encouraged. It must be understood that Satan will use anything and everything good or bad against us so that we won't believe in God, and he will definitely try to convince us to question any God at all that would let such sin into the world, which brings us back to the topic of free will. Remember free will is a freedom of choice given because we have our own spirit in order to be an individual. If someone should use free will for personal gain then it could possibly be at the expense of another individual, such as theft, abandonment or murder. When this occurs, naturally there will be people that wonder why God would allow such things and thus become mad at God, and Satan, of course, will use this to cause people to question whether there is indeed a God at all.

This is an important subject to talk about because so many have been caught up in this trap. First of all, Satan uses the very free will that makes us an individual and a beauty all our own, for selfish gain thereby causing us to sin against God and our fellow man. But then Satan gets people to blame God for the very sin that he convinced us to commit. For example, let's look at the story of Adam and Eve. Satan caused them to sin and what was their response to the question when God asked them why they did it?

Genesis 3:12

> *The man said, "The woman you put here with me - she gave me some fruit from the tree, and I ate it."*

Emphasis on "The woman YOU put here". There it is. Clear as ever. Satan convinced them to sin and then helped the man to blame God. The gift of free will was given by God as a means to enhance our lives but Satan would have you believe that once you sinned, or someone sinned against you, that it's God's fault. It's not God's fault so let us put the blame back where blame belongs. Yes, you could argue that God allowed it to happen so it must be his fault, but remember God gave us free will and for him to stop free will would be to stop our individuality, not to mention our ability to turn away from our sin back to the loving arms of God. If you were given the ability to turn from sin shouldn't other people have the same ability? Remember, it is not our place to determine whose sin is greater or lesser and who deserves heaven or hell because we have not the ability to see into another person's heart.

The "Individual Time" discussed previously is a tactic that Satan used and uses against the believer as well. For example, when someone is busy building their life the way they wish then they are not open to the direction of God, nor are they open to any true understanding of what is important to God or what matters most. They will constantly be creating for their own personal gain while asking God to help them in their goals. They cease to ask what God wants or if it is okay with him. And if that someone should become successful, then they will drift slowly away from God and acknowledge him less and less. Their personal time with God will become less important and the relationship will suffer. If enough time is spent working on things that we deem necessary, then God is forgotten. Therefore time becomes a very important topic because time used unwisely and not spent with God will bring an eventual loss in the strength of our knowledge of, and personal relationship with, God. Thus, selfish tendencies will rise and sin becomes more prevalent.

Remember, Satan has worked patiently through time to build a body of lies to work against the creation so that it is very hard to see the loving

God that stands before it. Over time Satan has so twisted the ideas of mankind that we have come to believe what is good is difficult and what is evil is desirable.

Today sinful living appears exciting and glamorous.

Satan would have us believe that sin is fun but in reality sin brings a degradation of the heart causing a sadness of spirit. God did not make us to enjoy sin so only when a heart is repented does the soul rejoice.

The problem is we no longer look at the long term effects of our actions but rather the immediate response or gain. Again, it's a time factor. If an action brings forth immediate gratification then we are more apt to take the step, sin or not. It is important to understand that Satan will ask us to take an immediate gratification for ourselves which will come at a long-term cost, whereas God would have us give an immediate cost to ourselves that yields long-term gratification. Let me explain. When Satan asks us to sin by caring for ourselves, that selfish action could be at the expense of another human being, though it definitely is at the expense of our own heart as stated above. But if God asks us to give to another human being which has a need, that little but of love shown could bring forth great rewards later. Selfishness begets selfishness, love begets love.

If you sacrifice your time, money and love for your children to better their opportunities, you will have a wonderful relationship and love of family later on in life. If you show the love and care for a sick child while they are in your care and later you should become sick yourself, the odds are that same grown-up child will be caring for you in your time of need, not to mention the love and respect you will have for one another throughout the years.

The greatest example we have of this spirit of heart is the life of Jesus. He gave of himself throughout his life by healing the sick, giving sight to the blind and showing love to the loveless. And then he gave his life completely on the cross which had an immediate and painful cost, but look at the long-term advantage it brings. Not only does it pay for our sin so that we may live with God but it brings a loving relationship between God and man once again. Of course this is an extreme example but the point is that as love is given, so love is received.

Okay, so let's say you are a Christian that is trying to believe and live a life according to the will of God. Well, Satan then uses other tactics to bring forth a dilution of deity in your life.

Accusations

In the book of Revelation in chapter twelve verse ten it calls Satan the "Accuser". Understand that Satan will try to accuse anything and everything to us. If a person becomes too busy with life (that time factor again) and doesn't take the time to spend with God, which brings a proper understanding of heart, then their heart is more open to the traps, snares and in this case the accusations of Satan.

The Accuser will use this tactic of suggestions because, as time has shown, it is successful in playing one person, or a whole organization, against another. For example, if two people were in a conversation and one said something that could be misunderstood or misinterpreted and the other went home and began to dwell on it negatively, then they need to be careful because Satan will use this opportunity to accuse the other person. If that person should become angry with the misinterpreted person without giving them the opportunity to explain, then it becomes sin because the other person never meant to cause any harm.

Complete relationships, even Christian relationships, have been lost because one or both listened to what we'll call "Satan Suggestions". If Satan can suggest to one that another is against them and they accept it then that will become a problem between those two. And if Satan can work Christian against Christian then this becomes the primary focus instead of accomplishing God's command which is to go and make disciples of all nations.

The Accuser would have us condemn different aspects of the church, as if under a microscope, to the point that we are always accusing and never satisfied. If we have become content with one particular church then he will try to accuse all other churches of lacking any salvation at all, thereby our hearts disallow other churches of any purpose. And then the Accuser will even accuse to us the actions, dress and the interpretation and teachings from our pastors causing people to become disinterested and never content. If Satan can suggest something to someone this easily then he can keep them in a constant state of confusion, and thus slowing the progress of the message of Jesus.

But the most destructive suggestion of all has to be the accusations of self. After Satan tempts someone to sin he will accuse them to themselves and contends they are horrible.

In the story of Adam and Eve we find that after the temptation and sin they became disgusted with themselves and hid from God. The whole purpose of God creating us was to enjoy and cherish us; Satan wants the relationship destroyed so he not only tempts us to sin but afterward accuses us until we hide instead of turning our repented hearts back to God. If Satan can keep us from facing God then eventually we will become so calloused to our sin that we no longer search out the grace of God which causes us to live in a constant state of, as stated before, sadness of spirit.

Paul, knowing how Satan works and the concept of "Satan suggestions", wrote in Second Corinthians 10:5

We demolish arguments and every pretension that sets itself up against the knowledge of God, and we take captive every thought to make it obedient to Christ.

Influence

Another tactic of Satan's to dilute the deity is influence. Satan can and will introduce into our environment various words, ideas and mannerisms that allow us to slowly backslide into a calloused world that eventually resembles nothing of God or what is Godly. He will bring forth these coulters into our lives by way of family, friends, relationships or media in such a manner that it becomes the accepted, or the "norm". Satan would have us think that because everybody else is doing it that it must be okay.

So how does Satan influence us?

Probably the greatest influence we have, whether positive or negative is our **sight**. The very things we allow ourselves to see will cause a pictured memory that can be used by Satan to bring to the forefront of our minds at any time he chooses.

Matthew 6:22, 23

> *The eye is the lamp of the body. If your eyes are good, your whole body will be full of light. But if your eyes are bad, your whole body will be full of darkness. If then the light within you is darkness, how great is that darkness!*

Television is probably the greatest form of visual influence that we have available to us. Most of us will sit down after a tiresome day and just watch as our minds are filled with what the media determines. We will be bombarded with commercials, shows and news broadcasts depicting the evidence of what the world has become as the commercials and shows advocate sexual content whereas the shows and news broadcasts advocate violence. The more we watch this influence the more it becomes an accepted understanding and way of life.

This will carry over onto our movies and in fact the movie moguls have been given more freedom in which to prejudice our minds. Depending on the movie we determine will allow us more violence, more nudity and even the beliefs of what we come to stand by. There are movies of the heart and movies of hatred, movies of peace and movies of war, movies of God and movies of magical powers of mortal man. Depending upon the movie and the director's agenda these movies can either bring us to visualize the greatness of God or it can be used to dilute his strength by bringing God down or raising man up.

But what if a convicted mind should take the steps necessary to command more control over what they see? Well, they will still have to contend with the subject of clothing. If selfishness is on the rise then loneliness is more prevalent. Couple that with the world's idea that "sex sells" and you will see more suggestive clothing in hopes for more attention. Bad or good, a young child will come to believe any attention is better than no attention at all. As that child's world spirals downward they will become more open to the world of pornography which will help them receive the attention and money they desire while the degradation of hearts and minds expands to a catastrophe. The world for both cast and audience becomes the way of lust opposing any real love at all, intentional or not.

Another way in which Satan will influence us is by **sound**. The right sound can be a soothing comfort or a constant contrast to the mood of our day. The sound of the beach can bring ease whereas the sound of traffic can bolster discomfort. One way in which sound can touch our lives is through music. The right use of music can soothe and comfort or motivate in spirit. Of course Satan's goal is to destroy the morality of man so he uses music to shock and degrade or introduce negative ideas and concepts. If lyrics degrading women or the use of extremely vulgar language are constantly pounding in our brains by way of a catchy beat then that message will better stay in our thoughts. Product salesmen have understood this fact for years. For example, how many jingles have we had stuck in our minds reminding us of a particular product?

As the sights and sounds around us introduce into our lives the very things that we were protected from previously then the conversations, jokes and even words will continue to bring forth a calloused comprehension of what is normal. Understandably as Satan works to degrade our concept of what is right and wrong then the children will be influenced by the calloused elder, whether parent, sibling or friend.

If those that have no morals are teaching the moral then morality is lost. Understand that a world Satan is slowly influencing into a non-Godly condition would not have in it the things that would please God. When morality is brought down then the way of life and love is lost. **Lives will become more individualized allowing Satan to work on each, unprotected and without strength.**

The need for mankind to try to find a way to escape from the world in which they now live becomes paramount to any kind of survival. Souls that naturally longed to be loved by the one that created them will search out some kind of **"Vice"** to either stop the pain of reality or subdue it for the time being. Satan will try to counter this move by way of drugs, alcohol, movies, sex, relationships or even suicide. The problem lies in that the soul needs to be loved but the world has become more selfish and therefore hearts are lost.

Does this sound more like hell than earth?

Truth is… yes. We discussed previously that heaven would be a place with total God, or total love, whereas hell would be a place with total lack of God, or total selfishness. As Satan has worked over many years to slowly dilute the deity he has accomplished a decline in morality and the truth in the strength of the love that God has for us to call upon.

The disciples understood the direction of the world and how Satan works which led John to write in First John 2:15, 16

> *Do not love the world or anything in the world. If anyone loves the world, the love of the Father is not in him. For everything in the world - the cravings of sinful man, the lust of his eyes and the boasting of what he has and does-comes not from the Father but from the world.*

Please understand:

The lack of proper use of personal time and the way in which Satan will work it against us will cause a dilution of deity in our **Heart**.

Listening to "Satan suggestions" will cause a dilution of deity in our **Soul**.

And influences through worldly things, whether sight, sound or vices will cause a dilution of deity that will diminish any **Strength**.

And what was the most important command given by God?

Deuteronomy 6:5

> *Love the Lord your God with all your **heart** and with all your **soul** and with all your **strength**.*

When God gave us this commandment it was not a selfish request but an understanding of how the mind works and what the heart desires. God is truly the creator and set the boundaries that would help us to live a wonderful and loving experience, but Satan knows this all too well and therefore works to make it complicated.

Matthew 14:25-31

> *During the fourth watch of the night Jesus went out to them, walking on the lake. When the disciples saw him walking on the lake, they were terrified. "It's a ghost," they said, and cried out in fear. But Jesus immediately said to them: "Take courage! It is I. Don't be afraid."*
>
> *"Lord, if it's you." Peter replied, "tell me to come to you on the water."*
>
> *"Come," he said.*
>
> *Then Peter got down out of the boat, walked on the water and came toward Jesus. But when he saw the wind, he was afraid and, beginning to sink, cried out, "Lord, save me!"*

Immediately Jesus reached out his hand and caught him. "You of little faith," he said, "why did you doubt?"

When Simon Peter witnessed Jesus walking on the water he was caught up in the moment and removed temporarily from the understandings of this earth. He then called upon Jesus and was able to do what few men have done, but when Satan reminded him of where he was and what he was doing his eyes were removed from God's understanding and he saw only the ways of the world once again, thus he began to believe that he was unable to do that which he was indeed doing, and he began to sink.

Simon Peter walked on water.

Satan made it complicated.

4

Does God Find You Important?

The most damaging lies that Satan would have you believe is that you are just not good enough for God; that he could never forgive you; that your sins are much too disastrous for God's kingdom; and in extreme cases, that not even God could love you. This kind of thinking brings a tear to God's heart because he made you. God has an absolute love for you and he proved it by committing the greatest act of love known when he put himself on the cross to save you. But that has been stated so many times in life that it has become unfathomable. Satan would still have you believe that it doesn't apply to you. So let's look at scriptures to see just how important you are to God.

First let's look at an example of God's compassion.

Compassion: a deep understanding sympathy of someone's suffering accompanied by a longing to alleviate that suffering.

In the book of John we read the story of a man named Lazarus who had become ill and it didn't look favorable so word was sent to Jesus to come and help. Jesus was known for his ability to heal the sick especially by his friends that had witnessed these miracles. Mary, Martha and their brother Lazarus were good friends of Jesus and in fact scriptures say in John chapter eleven verse five that he loved them, so they were not unaware of his abilities. The story continues to express that while Jesus was still far away Lazarus had died so when Jesus arrived Lazarus had already been in his tomb four days.

John 11:32-35

> *When Mary reached the place where Jesus was and saw him, she fell at his feet and said, "Lord, if you had been here, my brother would not have died."*
>
> *When Jesus saw her weeping, and the Jews who had come along with her also weeping, he was deeply moved in spirit and troubled. "Where have you laid him?" he asked.*
>
> *"Come and see, Lord," they replied.*
>
> *Jesus wept.*

This scripture continues to say that Jesus went up to the tomb, had them remove the stone that sealed it and then raised Lazarus from the dead. All was well. Everything was as it was before. So this brings forth the question: If Jesus knew that he was about to raise Lazarus from the dead and that in just a few patient moments Lazarus would be with his sisters once again, why did he weep?

Jesus, knowing he had the power to raise Lazarus from the dead, could have simply said to Mary, "There's no need for tears. I'm going to bring him back, you'll see." But Jesus didn't and in fact we read that he cried. This could simply suggest only one thing: that Jesus was deeply moved when he witnessed the emotional sorrow of a dear friend who was in mourning for the loss of her brother. Yes, Jesus knew it would all be over in just a few moments and he knew that there would in fact be elation, but it didn't alleviate the broken hearts of the unknowledgeable people around him in that moment, so it touched him to tears. This story shows Jesus as compassionate.

Okay, one could argue that this is a story about someone he loved. And you're right, it clearly states in John that he loved them. But this does not tell us that he doesn't love us, and in fact the story of the cross tells us that he does. This part of the story only determines that Jesus has a compassionate heart insomuch that even when everything will conclude all right, he cries when we cry.

So as we look to other stories of Jesus, what does it say about love and compassion for people that he didn't spend time with, or people that he just met?

Luke 7:12-15

> *As he approached the town gate, a dead person was being carried out-*
> *the only son of his mother, and she was a widow. And a large crowd*
> *from the town was with her. When the lord saw her, his heart went*
> *out to her and he said, "Don't cry." Then he went up and touched the*
> *coffin, and those carrying it stood still. He said, "Young man, I say to*
> *you, get up!" The dead man sat up and began to talk, and Jesus gave*
> *him back to his mother.*

We see in this story that Jesus and his disciples, while traveling to a new location, had happened upon a funeral procession. It states the person that had died was *"the only son of his mother, and she was a widow."* This is very important to the story because it shows the desperation of the woman's life. True, the reason this story is in the Bible is because Jesus had raised someone from the dead, but it was strictly a moment of compassion that compelled Jesus to perform such a miraculous act.

Understand that in ancient times a woman did not work outside the home unless she was unscrupulous, and it was up to the son to care for a widowed mother. This woman had already lost her husband and now life had dealt her an overwhelming loss. This woman's life as she knew it was over and it would leave her with questions of uncertainty for the future.

This quiet little story is one whose meaning could easily be bypassed because it is not depicting a God that is trying to impress upon the disciples a need for them to believe in the power at his command and that he is indeed God, but rather a simple witness of how God understood this woman's situation and out of love and compassion took away all devastating loss. The final cap to the story is that after Jesus had raised the young man he *"gave him back to his mother."* In other words, he gave back her life, love and livelihood. The strongest point to this story is not that Jesus had raised someone from the dead, although that is a miraculous act, but the written words *"his heart went out to her and he said, 'Don't cry.'"* This is a total act of love and compassion even for someone he had just met.

All right, one could still argue that these stories were of kind and caring people that didn't deserve to suffer. After all, it doesn't tell us the nature of the heart of each of these people Jesus showed compassion for.

And Satan would have us look beyond the love demonstrated in these stories to see ourselves only as non-forgivable. Remember his nickname is the Accuser which tells us that after tempting us into sin he will torment us into believing we are the absolute worst and that God's love was not meant for us.

So let us now read scripture depicting a meeting of Jesus and a person that we clearly see is not living a life of morality. In fact she is an outcast. But first it is important to understand the history of the times to fully grasp the totality of this story.

Understand that ancient beliefs considered this to be a man's world. The woman was strictly to serve the man, and children were of course waiting to grow up and take their place in society.

Man was to rule over all things and the Jews, being the "Chosen Ones" of God, considered themselves to be over all men. What does it mean to be the chosen one? In ancient times when the world had become decadent, God found and tested one man who was good. Because this man was obedient God made a pact with him that as long as he and his offspring obeyed God they would flourish in all they did, which would then show the rest of the world that they honored and obeyed the one and only true God. This, in turn, would help the world be directed back to the God which Satan had worked so hard to discredit. Of course history tells us that they did not stay in obedience to God so as their sins progressed God stepped back and let other nations conquer and at times even enslave them.

Now if the Jews considered themselves to be the hierarchy over all men then this allows the Pharisees and Sadducees to be of the greatest position for they were above all Jewish men. In the Jewish community the only person that would be above the Pharisees and Sadducees would be any one of the Prophets and of course above them would be the Messiah himself.

Herein lies a problem because the Jews were at this time under Roman rule. They truly believed that if and when the Messiah came he would set everything straight to their understanding.

So let us recap. In the Jewish community the proper order of mankind would be:

1. Pharisees and Sadducees
2. Jews
3. All other men including the Romans
4. Women
5. And then children.

If you were a Samaritan, which the Jews hated, you would then be placed at the lowest of the order and the Samaritan women would be the absolute bottom. A Samaritan was considered to be an outcast by all Jews.

So what was a Samaritan and why were they hated by the Jews?

King Omri (an appointed king of Israel) bought a hill for two talents of silver and built his city on it. He named his capital to the northern kingdom of Israel Samaria, which eventually referred to the entire district of the northern kingdom. By this time the Israelites had become split into two kingdoms: the northern kingdom, still called the Israelites, and the southern kingdom consisting of the half tribe of Benjamin and the tribe of Judah, now known as the Jews.

In 722 B.C. the king of Assyria had taken captive the territory of the Israelites (the northern kingdom) and moved most of the population of the ten northern tribes out and transported many non-Israelites into Samaria. This was a common practice of a conquering king, to bring down the inner strength by diluting the race of the captives. Even though God had forbidden intermarriage, they eventually did marry to form a mixed race to which a tension and eventual hatred had developed between the returning Jews and the people now called Samaritans.

So now the list would appear:

1. Pharisees and Sadducees
2. Jews
3. All other men including the Romans
4. Women
5. Children
6. Samaritans

Understanding this we are now able to determine just how important, strong and wonderful is the story of Jesus and the woman at the well.

John 4:5-26.

> *So he came to a town in Samaria called Sychar, near the plot of ground Jacob had given to his son Joseph. Jacob's well was there, and Jesus, tired as he was from the journey, sat down by the well. It was about the sixth hour.*
>
> *When a Samaritan woman came to draw water, Jesus said to her, "Will you give me a drink?" (His disciples had gone into the town to buy food.)*
>
> *The Samaritan woman said to him, "You are a Jew and I am a Samaritan woman. How can you ask me for a drink?" (For Jews do not associate with Samaritans.)*
>
> *Jesus answered her, "If you knew the gift of God and who it is that asks you for a drink, you would have asked him and he would have given you living water."*
>
> *"Sir," the woman said, "you have nothing to draw with and the well is deep. Where can you get this living water? Are you greater than our father Jacob, who gave us the well and drank from it himself, as did also his sons and his flocks and herds?"*
>
> *Jesus answered, "Everyone who drinks this water will be thirsty again, but whoever drinks the water I give him will never thirst. Indeed, the water I give him will become in him a spring of water welling up to eternal life."*
>
> *The woman said to him, "Sir, give me this water so that I won't get thirsty and have to keep coming here to draw water."*
>
> *He told her, "Go, call your husband and come back."*
>
> *I have no husband," she replied.*
>
> *Jesus said to her, "You are right when you say you have no husband. The fact is, you have had five husbands, and the man you now have is not your husband. What you have just said is quite true."*
>
> *"Sir," the woman said, "I can see that you are a prophet. Our fathers worshiped on this mountain, but you Jews claim that the place where we must worship is in Jerusalem."*

Jesus declared, "Believe me, woman, a time is coming when you will worship the Father neither on this mountain nor in Jerusalem. You Samaritans worship what you do not know; we worship what we do know, for salvation is from the Jews. Yet a time is coming and has now come when the true worshipers will worship the Father in spirit and truth, for they are the kind of worshipers the Father seeks. God is spirit, and his worshipers must worship in spirit and in truth."

The woman said, "I know that Messiah" (called Christ) "is coming. When he comes, he will explain everything to us."

Then Jesus declared, "I who speak to you am he."

When reading this story it is easy to just read it and move on wondering why it is placed in the Bible. It's a quaint little story of Jesus and a woman in a conversation whereby she eventually becomes excited and runs off to tell the town that she has just met a man that could be the Messiah. Simple! That is until you take a closer look. Then it becomes a beautiful story expressing just how much God loves and accepts his creation. We can't hide our sins from God. He knows everything about us. So with this let us look deeply into this story and reveal God's heart.

First of all it was a common practice for women to gather in groups when they came to draw water, and then they would come in the early morning or late afternoon to avoid the sun's heat. But here we read that a woman came to draw water around noon and she came alone. This may be an indication of public shame that has caused her to be isolated from other women, which would indicate her as a social outcast. Being that a Samaritan would be a Jewish outcast this would make her an outcast of outcasts.

The list of Jewish order would now appear like this:

1. Messiah
2. Prophets
3. Pharisees and Sadducees
4. Jews
5. All other men including the Romans
6. Women
7. Children

8. Samaritans (outcasts)

9. Samaritan women

10. Woman at the well (outcast of outcasts)

When the story begins we see Jesus ask a Samaritan woman for a drink of water. It was unacceptable for a man of these times to talk to a woman, much less a Jewish man to talk to a Samaritan woman, which explains the woman's confusion when she replied, *"You are a Jew and I am a Samaritan woman. How can you ask me for a drink?"*

This woman had accepted her status as an outcast of outcasts so if anyone should converse with her it would be a highlight in her day. To this woman Jesus was fourth on the social list and she was tenth so when Jesus began talking with her, although confusing to her, it was an action of immediate acceptance. Not even the females of her race had done that. Jesus was exhibiting the characteristics of divine, indiscriminate love; the heart of a true creator.

Jesus then begins to introduce himself through a series of statements to help her past the worldly understandings, but since the woman failed to comprehend the nature of the "Living Water" Jesus then turns the conversation to a more personal matter.

"Go, call your husband and come back."

This woman was suddenly brought back to her own accepted reality when she was faced with answering the statistics of her life and the circumstances of shame. Her heart fell. Jesus had made her feel as if the status of one's place in society was unimportant as he conversed with her. Now all she could offer up was a quiet *"I have no husband"* for in her mind she saw herself as unequal once again. But Jesus alleviated this shame of status when he said to her, *"You are right when you say you have no husband. The fact is, you have had five husbands, and the man you now have is not your husband. What you have just said is quite true."*

The point of Jesus was not to shame her but help her to realize the love and acceptance of the almighty God who would send a Messiah to pay for the sins of the world, including hers. He is showing her that he not only accepted her as they talked, which would enable her to feel, if but for a moment, as though she were not an outcast of outcasts, but that he knew everything about her and still continued to converse. Suddenly joy was upon her, coupled with an awareness of the person there amongst her. This was obviously no ordinary man.

"Sir, I can see that you are a prophet,"

she states in an excited manner as she then begins to ask the intrigues of her heart to better understand what is right in the eyes of God, to which Jesus then offers up the answers of understanding.

In her mind Jesus has just been raised to the second status, whereas she is at the tenth but her starvation for knowledge of God compels her to converse in comfort as Jesus continues to guide her excitement to a better comprehension of God.

Realize to her this was an important man of God in her presence and he has made her feel comfortable enough to actually talk as if they were lifelong friends. This woman has never felt this way. She was used to being considered the bottom of the realm and right now she was privileged to live, if but for a moment, in a world where the social status was of no importance. If indeed a Prophet, the importance of this man could tell her most things, so in her elation she brings up the Messiah.

"I know that Messiah" (called Christ) *"is coming. When he comes, he will explain everything to us."*

A reader can almost hear the softness in her voice and see the joy in her eyes as she expresses this, to which Jesus drops one final declaration when he states,

"I who speak to you am he."

It is important to understand that in this woman's thoughts Jesus has gone, in just a very short time of conversation, from the fourth position to the extreme top of the social order. And this is that very same social order in which only a moment ago she saw herself as the lowest.

Before her was the Messiah, and in his love and compassion he placed himself beneath her. When the rest of the world saw her as unworthy, Jesus saw her as someone special. And she felt it so much that she then ran off to the very people that had considered her the outcast to tell of the great love in their midst. He went on to prove his love by placing himself on the cross to pay for the very sins that he already knew of, for example this woman, and for all future sins as well. He placed all mankind before himself in that commanding act of sacrifice.

That's how important each and every one of us is to God.

John 3:16

> *For God so loved the world that he gave his one and only Son, that whoever believes in him shall not perish but have eternal life.*

5

How Personal is Your Relationship with God?

In the beginning God created mankind and placed them in the Garden of Eden where they had need for nothing. Everything was set in God's order and man was able to live amongst God. But we learned that as Satan tempted free will man accepted, sinned and turned his back on God. Therefore, God put them out of the Garden to toil in a new world filled with good and evil, love and selfishness. Everything now was no longer under God's order but had become a world of chaos.

As things are now in a state of chaos, Christians are bound to receive some type of emotional pain as they live among the ideas and principles of this world. We as Christians, just because we know the truth about God and try to live accordingly, does not mean we are immune to the chaos around us. If enough darts are thrown in our direction we are bound to be hit eventually. We will have spouses that leave us, families that abandon us, friends that use us and loved ones that pass away. Therefore we will end up hurt or damaged from the lives we are intertwined with. The more life we have lived the more dents to our hearts we will receive. That's just the way of chaos.

You can't make your spouse love you.

You can't keep a loved one from passing.

You can't even make another person see beyond their own little world.

Mankind is strong so we will find a way for some sort of relief. We will surround ourselves amongst friends with similar personalities. We will allow ourselves the solitude of our homes and we will bury ourselves in hobbies to keep from exposing our lives to any pain. But this is just a temporary relief because the selfishness of this world will find a way to touch our lives. You can't hide from it.

So what can be done to survive?

Well, a body of believers can gather in order to encourage one another, support one another, serve one another and strengthen one another and the church has become just such a place. If we gather every Saturday or Sunday to participate in some kind of action with other fellow Christians then we will cover the pain and sorrow we feel and help our hearts to make it through another week.

The importance of the church is to teach the world of the salvation and grace offered us, to allow for the needy, to encourage counsel and to provide fellowship, worship and strength of words. The church will also provide the tools we can use that will expose any lies that Satan would have us believe in order to stop the progress of truth that God would have us learn. Knowing this, Christians will search out different churches to find just the right group of people and just the right pastor to help them meet their ideas, principles and that particular way for them to survive.

So what if we want more than just to survive from the dents to our hearts? What if we want to heal from those wounds to live a more complete and fuller life?

After all God said he would fill our lives with Joy, right? But most Christians, after going through a crisis, divorce or loss, find themselves asking "where is the Joy?"

Acts 16:23-25

> *After they had been severely flogged, they were thrown into prison, and the jailer was commanded to guard them carefully. Upon receiving such orders, he put them in the inner cell and fastened their feet in the stocks. About midnight Paul and Silas were praying and singing hymns to God, and the other prisoners were listening to them.*

In this story the apostle Paul and Silas express great joy right after they had been beaten, flogged and placed into stocks, which are very uncomfortable. They could easily have been complaining to God about their circumstances but instead they were singing praises to him.

Question: How were they able to have such joy in an obvious painful experience?

Answer… **It's a matter of the heart.**

In chapter three we discussed how sin brings a degradation of heart causing a sadness of spirit, and that God did not make us to enjoy sin so only when a heart is repented does the soul rejoice. Paul and Silas had repented hearts so the pain they felt was a physical pain and not the deep emotional pain of spirit. Even when the outside world was violent their souls were filled with Joy. The difference then becomes what we allow into our hearts.

When we came to believe in God we were told to confess our sins and accept God into our hearts. So what exactly does that mean? Well, to confess our sins means that we are truly sorry for the wrongs that we have committed against God and mankind so with an apologetic heart we ask God for his forgiveness. But we can't just say to God "Please forgive me of my sins" and move on, hoping for our lives to change while hanging on to the very ways which affected our hearts in the first place. True, the feeling of having our sins removed from us brings on a great relief but you have to let go of your life completely, otherwise you will find yourself struggling with the same sins over and over.

Understand that it's the weakness of trying to hang onto who we are and the rights we feel we deserve that Satan uses against us.

John 12:25a

The man who loves his life will lose it.

Matthew 10:39

Whoever finds his life will lose it, and whoever loses his life for my sake will find it.

You have to give your life completely over to God as he has given himself to you. God doesn't just meet us at church. He provided a way in which to always live with us for he gave the Holy Spirit to live within us. If we have repented our lives and given them to God then we have accepted God into our hearts. Therefore God lives in us.

John 14:15-17

> *"If you love me, you will obey what I command. And I will ask the Father, and he will give you another Counselor to be with you forever - the Spirit of truth. The world cannot accept him, because it neither sees him nor knows him. But you know him, for he lives with you and will be in you."*

If God is in us then why at times do we still have a sadness of spirit? Well, because we are still allowing other things (sins) into our hearts besides God.

So what could be the sins affecting our hearts?

When people try to accept God on their own terms and hang onto the life they feel they deserve then their relationship with God only grows to a point and then plateaus. When this happens they will find themselves struggling with the same snare or trap and will succumb to the same sins again and again and again.

As we accept God into our lives God will take us though stages of growth. The first of these stages is acceptance, repentance and commitment. The second is obedience.

John 14:23, 24

> *If anyone loves me, he will obey my teaching. My Father will love him, and we will come to him and make our home with him. He who does not love me will not obey my teaching. These words you hear are not my own; they belong to the Father who sent me.*

When people accept God on their own terms and are not fully committed then they end up spending the rest of their lives fighting this second stage. They never get past it. They are caught in a cycle of obedience, disobedience, repentance and then back to obedience again. This will cause the sadness of spirit as discussed before and thereby creates an inner turmoil of conflicting suffering. Their whole life will be of highs and lows in their walk with God. Every time they repent their hearts will rejoice but as soon as they fall to the same sin their spirit will suffer a deep emotional sorrow.

The Accuser (Satan) will play upon this to his advantage. He will continuously make this person feel as low as possible so that they hide from God. If he can cause them to hide long enough then they will become calloused to their sin, give up and just accept it as part of their life. But should the person continue to try to please God but never fully release their life to him then the problem will persist and in some cases Satan will cause the suffering to expand and thus bring forth belief that they can never get past it so the only way of relief is suicide.

Understand that a non-believer is one that would put themselves first, others second and God last because they don't believe in God, and the Christian that believes but on their own terms will still put themselves first but God second and others last. The only thing that has changed is that God has moved up one position. Let me show this in a chart.

Group	First	Second	Third
Non-Believer	themselves	others	God
Christian (on their terms)	themselves	God	others

It is apparent that with both groups they are still putting themselves first. Therefore the only thing this Christian has gained is the salvation of God but they never really experience the relationship he has to offer as they continually suffer from their sins.

This type of Christian is subject to the deep emotional pain inflicted upon them from someone else's sins as well because they put themselves first so they unknowingly hang onto any heartfelt pain. It's all about them. If someone they have trusted should hurt them it becomes very difficult to move on and live the life God had intended, and in some cases they relive the pain for years afterwards.

The Christian of their own terms will expect God to forgive their sins, but will be more apt to hold the very sins that someone else has committed against them. They may be mad at God for a loved one's passing. They may refuse to forgive someone who hurt them because of the need to see that other person suffer with their own eyes. And they may still blame their spouse for leaving them. Remember this Christian places themselves first, therefore they will hold the attitude of "you hurt me and now you need to pay" in their hearts.

This Christian will call out to God for justice. The very same justice they hope God doesn't deliver upon them for their sins. When God does not produce justice in their timing then they will take matters into their own hands for they feel justice should be administered. This will cause them to fight in court to make sure the offending party receives nothing that they worked so hard as a team to create. They will fight for child custody not because they really want the children but it becomes a way to make the other pay for the abandonment they now feel. And of course they will flaunt any court winnings in front of the opposing spouse. All this while rationalizing their sins by comparing themselves against the world and believing that they have certain unalienable rights so therefore they should be able to make the other suffer for the pain they have caused.

How can they justify pain for others, whether they deserve it or not, if by God's grace they have escaped conviction of their own sins? Do they truly comprehend that any present pain is short lived for life on earth is only temporary? Is this the mark of a person that truly loves God?

Luke 6:41

> *Why do you look at the speck of sawdust in your brother's eye and pay no attention to the plank in your own eye?*

The sad part is when the non-believer witnesses how bad one Christian can treat another, then of course their reaction becomes one of "I don't want any part of that" or "what makes them any different than me?" So you can see why we have all heard the comment "Christians are hypocrites", and Satan will use this as a way to keep the non-believer from having any part of God at all. Thus, in our selfishness we are allowing Satan to keep others from the very salvation that we will enjoy when the end times arrive.

John 13:34

> *A new command I give you: Love one another. As I have loved you, so you must love one another. By this all men will know that you are my disciples, if you love one another.*

If the God of love and mercy truly lives in our hearts then how can the pain of the past still be there? Understand that as long as we hold onto self and don't let God have control of our hearts then we are vulnerable to any pain that another, who chooses not to walk with God, can administer. You have to let go and let God fill your heart completely. This will help you grow with God, spiritually, physically, mentally and emotionally and thereby help you to become Godly. Being Godly is to try to live according to God's principles.

Therefore a Godly person is one that puts God first, others second and themselves last.

Group	First	Second	Third
Non-Believer	themselves	others	God
Christian (on their terms)	themselves	God	others
Godly	God	others	themselves

Now you can see in this chart that God has moved up to the first position and self has moved to the very last. This places others before oneself and thereby becomes a pattern of living in humility and servitude.

When one truly views themselves in this manner then they are less open for the pain of deep emotional hurt that another can cause because they will not hang onto any pain in their heart. God lives in their heart and if God fills their heart then love will fill their heart for God is love. This will bring on a proper understanding and attitude of God, others and self and because of this, healing occurs.

Forgiveness

When we allow ourselves to become Godly, once we have had our feelings hurt we are more apt not to judge another, for we remember that we ourselves have sinned. We will take our heartaches to God and let him comfort us instead of trying to carry out vengeance ourselves. We will adopt the attitude that what they did is between them and God and we will in fact pray that God forgives them and doesn't cast them into the fires of hell. Thanks to God no pain that we receive will last, so the idea of someone paying for any partial pain through all eternity is just unfathomable. We will be more focused upon appreciating the love and compassion that God has shown than the partial pain administered by another's selfish act.

Forgiveness is not just for the person that committed the sin but for the forgiver as well, for forgiveness cleanses the heart of any ungodly emotions and allows for healing. So healing begins when forgiveness starts and no sooner.

Freedom

As we become Godly we receive freedom from the continuous circling sin that grips us from ever reaching a personal relationship with God. We no longer are trapped in a revolving door of commitment, sin, repentance and commitment as before, but become more concerned about obedience which allows freedom for God to grow within us, thus our relationship with God grows. We no longer are slaves to any vices that Satan has convinced us we need in order to hide from the reality of life we are striving so hard to escape from. We no longer are locked in continuous pain from loss or abandonment and we are no longer trapped in a deep emotional heartfelt sorrow caused by the sadness of sin. Each day becomes easier not to sin, and when we do, it becomes a simple "God, I'm sorry, I didn't mean to do that. Please forgive me" and we move on knowing that God has indeed cleansed us from all unrighteousness.

Romans 6:6, 7

> *For we know that our old self was crucified with him so that the body of sin might be done away with, that we should no longer be slaves to sin - because anyone who has died has been freed from sin.*

Prayer

As we strive to live according to God's principles and therefore become Godly, prayer becomes the most important part of our life. Prayer brings closeness to God in a way that we can never receive just by reading the Bible. Don't get me wrong, the Bible is very important in learning as you fill your mind and heart with the instructions, comprehensions and examples of God. It brings forth a visual understanding of his life and teachings. But prayer allows for a personal communication between you and the creator of heaven and earth.

Therefore if prayer is this important there must be time set aside to encourage a more complete prayer life. One should pray at least thirty minutes every day and it should be in a place that allows freedom from interruptions. It also becomes more personal and more directed when you are speaking out loud to God as it allows for tears of sorrow or tears of joy. You will find that in the beginning you will have more pains and sorrows to address but later as your prayer life expands you will realize that you are praying more for others and less for any past pain or problems. As we spend time with God he is healing us from anything in our past and he is guiding us to and through our future.

As we pray he chides us to help keep us on the right path, for he wants no harm to come to us. He will instruct us so that we make the right choices in our different endeavors, he will comfort us if we should bring any emotional woes to him, he will listen to us as we bring different concerns to him, he will heal us of any deep heartfelt sorrows, he will reveal himself to us as we search for him, he will perform miracles for us because we simply came to him with a concern of someone's health, and he will cherish us and tell us that he loves us and is proud of us.

When all this happens, your heart begins to change and your attitude towards yourself naturally changes. Your attitude towards others will change as well and you will begin to see things in truth and understanding from God's point of view and not man's. You will begin to understand what is important and what will pass; what is proper and what is wrong; what is truth and what are lies. This will bring on a better understanding of the love of God and you will become content to help in whatever way you can to bring others to the arms of God.

You will find yourself saying to God "thanks for making my life less important", meaning that you have less of your life to bring to God because he has been watching over every part of it which then brings forth a freedom to pray and care for others.

John 15:9-12

> *As the Father has loved me, so have I loved you. Now remain in my love. If you obey my commands, you will remain in my love, just as I have obeyed my Father's commands and remain in his love. I have told you this so that my joy may be in you and that your joy may be complete. My command is this: Love each other as I have loved you.*

Herein lies the fulfillment of our hearts as we allow only what is Godly into our hearts. So it truly is **"a matter of the heart."**

6

Go Now and Leave Your Life of Sin

As we grasp the teachings and life of Jesus we learn through his example the disciplines and integrity that he would have our hearts achieve. He gave himself not only as a living example but also guided us to the importance of what God would have, contrasted against what man has, through Satan, given too much importance. Earlier in chapter two we discussed that Jesus came here to make sin less important. This means that once a sin is pointed out to us we simply confess our sins to God and with a contrite heart go and leave the sin behind. We cannot make the mistake of giving the sin too much importance. We have to let it go and let God become the importance in our heart and not the heaviness of sin.

This becomes a very important topic to discuss, for it is exactly the opposite of what Satan would have and what the world understands. The Accuser wishes only to keep us in our sins whether in sadness of spirit so that we hide from God or in action so that we never achieve growth. The Apostle Paul understood this, therefore he encourages us in his writings to reach for the example set by Jesus.

Romans 12:2a

> Do not conform any longer to the pattern of this world, but be transformed by the renewing of your mind.

2 Corinthians 2:11

In order that Satan might not outwit us. For we are not unaware of his schemes.

We as Christians need to become Godly and in order to do this we will need to learn discipline of the mind.

Discipline

The origin of the word comes from the Latin word disciplina which means instruction, which is derived from the root word discere which means to learn, and from which we also receive the word discipulus or disciple.

To live a disciplined life means to learn and administer a particular order of instruction to bring forth self-control that would produce a morally acceptable behavior. Not man's acceptable behavior but God's. For as we read in chapter three, Satan has spent many years producing an acceptable behavior in man that is warped and distorted beyond the boundaries of God.

The Law of Moses, instead of providing boundaries to the heart of God, had become an existence of sacraments and extended laws providing structure of command instead of growth of heart. When Jesus then began to teach the proper understanding of the Law the people became confused for it was not the way the teachers of the Law (the Pharisees and Sadducees) were expressing. There had become a lack of discipline of the heart. Thus we read that Jesus, while teaching a large crowd, explains his intentions in order to protect the Law and to provide comprehension to the true meaning of the Law.

Matthew 5:17

Do not think that I have come to abolish the Law or the Prophets; I have not come to abolish them but to fulfill them.

Matthew 5:20

For I tell you that unless your righteousness surpasses that of the Pharisees and the teachers of the law, you will certainly not enter the kingdom of heaven.

Understand that Jesus was teaching us to assemble individual laws of the heart in order to produce growth and enhance love, not structural laws that allow man the ability to keep order amongst men but still allow growth of selfishness. In other words, spiritual laws, not judicial laws, are what produce maximum growth. If a man allows himself a selfishness of the mind it then brings on moral decay of the heart causing man to commit a greater outward sin. Jesus clearly states that the selfishness of the mind is the true sin.

Matthew 5:21, 22a

> *You have heard that it was said to the people long ago, "Do not murder, and anyone who murders will be subject to judgment." But I tell you that anyone who is angry with his brother will be subject to judgment.*

Jesus is explaining that we will be judged by our hearts, not just the outward appearance we portray to others. Jesus reiterated this point that we may comprehend more fully.

Matthew 5:27, 28

> *You have heard that it was said, "Do not commit adultery." But I tell you that anyone who looks at a woman lustfully has committed adultery with her in his heart.*

Man will look to the outward committed sins whereas God views the wrongs we allow in our hearts as sin. A sin of the heart is a sin against God whereas an outward sin is a sin against mankind and God. Therefore if we have wrongful thoughts that we don't take hold of, it will cause us to sin against all.

Genesis 4:6, 7

> *Then the Lord said to Cain, "Why are you angry? Why is your face downcast? If you do what is right, will you not be accepted? But if you do not do what is right, sin is crouching at your door; it desires to have you but you must master it."*

Both in Genesis 4:7 *"sin is crouching at your door"* and Revelation 3:20 *"Here I am! I stand at the door and knock"* God uses the word "door" to represent our hearts. God is calling us to let him into our hearts to be filled with his joy and thus more complete, but he is also explaining that it's the wrongful inner thoughts that cause sin to take a controlling hold if allowed to continue, therefore we must master it in order to become Godly. Simply, we can either have God in our hearts or the selfish desires of sin.

Judicial laws, created to help produce order in a world of chaos, take into account the outer sins committed against one another such as murder, theft and adultery, but God is clearly stating that it first comes from an acceptance of selfishness within the heart. Temptation therefore comes from inside and leads to outward sin. Discipline is a way of clearing any potential growth of temptation, as discipline starts in the mind and conditions the heart. To adhere to discipline is to build character. The right character leads to integrity.

Integrity

Integrity is consistency of principles, actions, values and methods all of a higher standard produced from within. Having integrity means having a sense of honesty and morality that motivates a person's actions. This means that a person's heart is what drives them to do right. Therefore as we allow discipline to structure our minds we clearly build upon our hearts a sense of integrity that guides our lives.

Paul, in his letter to the Corinthians, is pleading for the believers to adhere to a particular comprehension that God takes precedence before all things.

I Corinthians 10:31

So whether you eat or drink or whatever you do, do it all for the glory of God.

This includes matters of the heart for where the heart goes so does the body. Therefore, as stated before, once the heart is repented that sin is to be discarded from your life. Do not give Satan the power of a victory because of sin.

The Apostle John writes in John 3:17

For God did not send his Son into the world to condemn the world, but to save the world through him.

If you fall to the temptations in life then you must repent, move on and allow God to cleanse you from within. If your heart and mind are kept clear of clutter allowing God to purify them, then he can grow within our hearts his wisdom, his truth and his love.

A great example of this can be found in the book of John where we read a story about the Pharisees bringing a woman caught in the act of sin and place her before Jesus. The Pharisees were not as concerned about the sin or upholding the Law of Moses as much as trying to use the Law in order to condemn Jesus. Their goal was to rid themselves of a concern that Jesus had become to their way of life. But as we read the story we see that Jesus takes care of the situation, disperses the crowd and then does something beautiful and miraculous.

John 8:2-11

> *At dawn [Jesus] appeared again in the temple courts, where all the people gathered around him, and he sat down to teach them. The teachers of the law and the Pharisees brought in a woman caught in adultery. They made her stand before the group and said to Jesus, "Teacher, this woman was caught in the act of adultery. In the Law Moses commanded us to stone such women. Now what do you say?" They were using this question as a trap, in order to have a basis for accusing him.*
>
> *But Jesus bent down and started to write on the ground with his finger. When they kept on questioning him, he straightened up and said to them, "If any one of you is without sin, let him be the first to throw a stone at her." Again he stooped down and wrote on the ground.*
>
> *At this, those who heard began to go away one at a time, the older ones first, until only Jesus was left, with the woman still standing there. Jesus straightened up and asked her, "Woman, where are they? Has no one condemned you?" "No one, sir," she said.*
>
> *"Then neither do I condemn you," Jesus declared. "Go now and leave your life of sin."*

The Pharisees felt they had thought this whole thing out. Jesus had become a problem for them for he was gathering more followers to his teachings every day and the Pharisees, Sadducees and the teachers of the Law who had enjoyed the prestige of their position were now finding an opposition to their standings. They figured by bringing this woman before the witness of a crowd and asking the advice of Jesus on the situation that either answer of yes or no would condemn him.

If Jesus out of compassion had said "No" to stoning her, the Pharisees could claim to the crowd that he is against Moses and the Law. Thereby he would lose the Jewish crowd of followers and his teachings would falter. The Pharisees and Sadducees, now having no opposition, would regain full control as another leader would be thwarted.

If Jesus had said "Stone her" which would be keeping the Law of Moses and thereby keeping the crowd of believers, the Pharisees could then have him turned over to the Romans for inciting a riot. The history between the Romans and the Jews had suffered many uprisings previously so for anyone to invoke a stoning, which is the taking of a life and a right the Romans believed exclusive, then the Romans would be forced to deal with the situation and have Jesus put to death. Again, problem solved for the Pharisees and Sadducees.

It is important to clarify that the Law clearly states that both the woman and the man be put to death for this act of sin.

Deuteronomy 22:22

> *If a man is found sleeping with another man's wife, both the man who slept with her and the woman must die. You must purge the evil from Israel.*

However, the teachers of the Law brought only the woman before Jesus, which further proves that they were not concerned about the Law of Moses but only to extinguish Jesus.

The downfall of the Pharisees started when they called Jesus "Teacher" in front of the crowd to induce his opinion. The Pharisees and Sadducees were of known higher position amongst the Jews so for the Pharisees to call him teacher is to admit to the gathering that he was a superior, a ranking of which they did not adhere to but it helped to start the entrapment of their ploy.

Note the contrast of hearts and actions that express exactly what we discussed previously. The Pharisees were living a life of structure that permitted or excluded certain actions to appear upright before the crowd, as opposed to the woman who was caught in the act of adultery so she would appear a sinner and thus shamed. The Pharisees saw themselves as above sin and thought themselves exclusive. They believed the right to take the life of this woman to further their advancement, whereas Jesus viewed their sin within. Their sins of the heart were about to become an outward sin at the expense of this woman.

The story continues when the opinion of Jesus was further pressed. He calmly stood up and with the statement *"if any one of you is without sin, let him be the first to throw a stone at her"* brought forth the reminder that none but God are without sin and that only God has the right to judge. Of course the elders were the first to leave for they would be more humbled of their sins, followed by the rest until only the woman remained standing before Jesus.

This woman knew not of Jesus but she knew the position of the Pharisees and they had called him teacher so she surmised that he must be of higher rank than they. Where the Pharisees viewed this woman as nothing and would use her to further their ploy at the expense of her very life, Jesus viewed her with value and showed mercy upon her. This becomes a great act of love.

This woman went from fear to confusion when suddenly she was left standing alone with this Teacher that had just dispersed the very crowd that would take her life. She knew she was guilty. She never even disputes it. She only stood silent before her accusers and now it appears that something was different.

When Jesus looked at the woman and spoke in quiet and comforting words *"Woman, where are they? Has no one condemned you?"* she, amazed by the situation that had just played out before her could only reply *"No one, sir."*

Compassionately Jesus spoke to her ***"Then neither do I condemn you."***

What powerful words.

It's interesting to note that we are not told of her story for that is not the importance of this story. We never read that Jesus sat her down and went over every little detail of how she became caught up in sin, but simply released her of her sin and sent her on her way with a new hope. The importance of this story becomes the value of which God places upon each and every one of us and the new start he gives us to move on and leave the sin behind.

In this story this woman was suddenly faced with something new that overshadowed her sin. She was left only to contemplate a new start and a new understanding of life, for this great teacher simply told her **"Go now and leave your life of sin."**

7

Go and Make Disciples

In ancient times God set up a nation that would be a witness to the rest of the world and bring an understanding of God to all people. But as we discussed before, the "Chosen Ones" had come to believe they were the only ones that would enter heaven and all others were bound for Sheol. The problem was that the decadence of man had progressed so badly that even the ones God had set up to obey his commands and become his example, had fallen from God's purpose. But even though they did not reach out to the rest of the world to proclaim God, we still see that through these "Chosen Ones" and the writings passed through their generations that an understanding of God did indeed reach out to all nations. Therefore even though they were disobedient God still fulfilled his purpose through them.

In the writings of this nation a Messiah had been foretold throughout the years by Prophets and the Psalms so by the time the Jews were under Roman repression the much anticipated Messiah was highly prayed for and hoped for. The Jews believed that when this Messiah came it would be only for the purpose of the Jews to restore the kingdom of the "Chosen Ones" to its full strength. They believed that this Messiah would come with power and great miraculous signs much like in the ancient times of Moses. But as we read the stories about Jesus, whom we now know as the Messiah, we see that he came with a servant's heart and a different purpose, which brought a reluctance of believers within the Jews for it was not the purpose that they had come to believe.

So what was the purpose of the Messiah?

Through the Israelites God brought us the Law of Moses so that structure of an outside order could provide growth of an inside order to our hearts. But before the times of Roman rule the Jews had already come to believe that if they followed the Law they could earn their way into heaven regardless of the sins in their hearts, but as Paul states in Romans 3:23

For all have sinned and fall short of the glory of God.

Therefore mankind cannot cleanse himself of sin by way of obedience to any Law and would thereby have to rely upon God for forgiveness. Thus the main purpose for the Messiah was to pay for the sins of man and save him from his own selfishness. God would also need to establish his church to reach out to all nations so that mankind may come to know and understand this salvation. Because of the misunderstanding of the Law another importance was that the Messiah needed to restore capabilities of the heart to bring a conscious choosing of love over selfishness.

Jesus was approximately thirty years of age when he started his ministry. As he began to pick out his disciples they immediately noticed a difference in the lifestyle and heart of Jesus so it's no surprise especially with the hope of the anticipated Messiah that we read of several comments concerning him stating he is the "Lamb of God", the "Messiah" or the "Son of God".

John 1:35, 36

The next day John was there again with two of his disciples. When he saw Jesus passing by, he said, "Look, the Lamb of God!"

John 1:40, 41a

Andrew, Simon Peter's brother, was one of the two who heard what John had said and who had followed Jesus. The first thing Andrew did was to find his brother Simon and tell him, "We have found the Messiah."

John 1:49

Then Nathanael declared, "Rabbi, you are the Son of God; you are the King of Israel."

It was with great hopes that they believed to have found their Messiah so their immediate response was to follow this "Rabbi", giving up their livelihood to become disciples of Jesus. When they first met Jesus it was apparent he was different so they commented and gave him a title of importance. But it was the progression of time and living with him day and night before the persuasiveness of just how right they were in their immediate assessments became prevalent.

Understand these men were mostly sea rugged, tough and strong physically and emotionally so their way of life and strength of character had to evolve to a love for all mankind as the ministry of Jesus progressed. Thus, he slowly advanced his teachings to bring forth a different understanding of the Messiah in contrast to the anticipated Messiah of the Jews.

John 14:6, 7

> *"I am the way and the truth and the life. No one comes to the father except through me. If you really knew me, you would know my father as well. From now on, you do know him and have seen him."*

Jesus began to show and teach that he and the Father were one. He provided them with a living example of the heart of the Father as time after time he showed them a compassion for others (even the ones that were considered outcasts, less important or sinners) as he healed the sick, gave sight to the blind and even gave life back to the dead.

Even with all the miracles that Jesus performed amongst them it's hard to grasp that the Messiah could actually be God and standing right in their very presence, thus, these mere men of the earth would still have moments of disbelief or even confusion.

In one instance as Jesus was teaching he began to explain a rather hard lesson that most of the crowd was unable to grasp so they began to leave one by one. Jesus then turned to the chosen Twelve and asked them if they too would leave.

John 6:67-69

> *"You do not want to leave too, do you?" Jesus asked the Twelve.*
>
> *Simon Peter answered him, "Lord, to whom shall we go? You have the words of eternal life. We believe and know that you are the Holy One of God."*

When Simon Peter stated *"to whom shall we go?"* it shows a changing within their hearts and a thirst of knowledge for a way of life that only Jesus would be able to fulfill. They could not even imagine anything else at this point for the disciples' love and dedication toward Jesus had became stronger with every passing day. But yet the questions would continue of just who this Jesus was that was teaching and performing miracles amongst them. The same questions arose within the religious leaders and the crowds that followed. Miracles were performed by Jesus out of compassion and mercy for the individual stated in the story, but some of the miracles were performed to convince the "Chosen Ones" that the time had arrived and their Christ was with them.

There were many discussions and rumors depicting Jesus with statements like "No one ever spoke the way this man does" and "When the Christ comes, will he do more miraculous signs than this man?" Jesus understood the doubts of the crowd but he could not allow a misdirection of the disciples. So we read in the book of Matthew that he brought forth questions in order to bring clearer the direction of their minds.

Matthew 16:13-17

> *When Jesus came to the region of Caesarea Philippi, he asked his disciples, "Who do people say the Son of Man is?"*
>
> *They replied, "Some say John the Baptist; others say Elijah; and still others, Jeremiah or one of the prophets."*
>
> *"But what about you?" he asked. "Who do you say I am?"*
>
> *Simon Peter answered, "You are the Christ, the Son of the living God."*
>
> *Jesus replied, "Blessed are you, Simon son of Jonah, for this was not revealed to you by man, but by my Father in heaven."*

This was important to be stated aloud as it strengthened their thoughts and helped to make sure that each of the disciples were guided in the same conclusion.

A short time later Jesus performed to comprehension in a way that they would never forget, how love dictates that you serve one another.

John 13:1

> *It was just before the Passover Feast. Jesus knew that the time had come for him to leave this world and go to the Father. Having loved*

his own who were in the world, he now showed them the full extent of his love.

John 13:4-14

So he got up from the meal, took off his outer clothing, and wrapped a towel around his waist. After that, he poured water into a basin and began to wash his disciples' feet, drying them with the towel that was wrapped around him.

He came to Simon Peter, who said to him, "Lord, are you going to wash my feet?"

Jesus replied, "You do not realize now what I am doing, but later you will understand."

"No," said Peter, "you shall never wash my feet."

Jesus answered, "Unless I wash you, you have no part with me."

"Then, Lord," Simon Peter replied, "not just my feet but my hands and my head as well!"

Jesus answered, "A person who has had a bath needs only to wash his feet; his whole body is clean. And you are clean, though not every one of you." For he knew who was going to betray him, and that was why he said not every one was clean.

When he had finished washing their feet, he put on his clothes and returned to his place. "Do you understand what I have done for you?" he asked them. "You call me 'Teacher' and 'Lord,' and rightly so, for that is what I am. Now that I, your Lord and Teacher, have washed your feet, you also should wash one another's feet."

This is an important powerful lesson for two reasons: First is that Jesus is using metaphorically the washing of feet to stress the point that in a world of indifference to God, we, as believers, can be clean of body and spirit but as we live upon this earth it will show us things that dilute the deity. As a bathed person gathers the dust of this earth upon their feet while walking, so does the spirit of heart gather the filth of the world of which we see and hear. It thereby becomes the duty of fellow Christians to help cleanse one another by way of support, instruction, provisions and love to provide growth of a proper heart of God.

The second reason was a proper understanding of love itself. God did not come here to be served and in fact we see in this instance, as in many others, he came to serve. But as the disciples' understanding of Jesus was becoming more powerful they would naturally want to place Jesus upon a higher realm, much like a king which was to be served, so it was hard for them to see their Lord place himself at the lowest of servants and wash their feet. Jesus was clearly expressing that when you love someone you will gladly serve that person, placing them before yourself to make sure that they are cared for.

Understand they were trying to hold within their thoughts the idea that this man was the "Anointed One of God" and yet here he was serving them as one who had no authority at all.

After three years of teaching and providing the disciples with a living example, Jesus knew the time for his primary reason had come, which was to give up his sinless life to pay for the sins of mankind. He knew of the events about to take place with his arrest, trial and crucifixion so he spent his last night in instruction so that once he had risen they would have strength of heart to carry on the work of creating churches to spread knowledge of the love of God to the very ends of the earth. He also knew that with the upcoming arrest they would become confused and lost in question for the next three days so he expressed three times the need for him to die.

John 12:23, 24

> Jesus replied, *"The hour has come for the Son of Man to be glorified. I tell you the truth, unless a kernel of wheat falls to the ground and dies, it remains only a single seed. But if it dies, it produces many seeds."*

The chief priests and elders performed the arrest in the early hours of the morning to keep the public that had come to believe in Jesus from thwarting their plans of eliminating him.

Matthew 26:47-54

> *While he was still speaking, Judas, one of the Twelve, arrived. With him was a large crowd armed with swords and clubs, sent from the chief priests and the elders of the people. Now the betrayer had arranged a signal with them: "The one I kiss is the man; arrest him." Going at once to Jesus, Judas said, "Greetings, Rabbi!" and kissed him. Jesus replied, "Friend, do what you came for."*

Then the men stepped forward, seized Jesus and arrested him. With that, one of Jesus' companions reached for his sword, drew it out and struck the servant of the high priest, cutting off his ear.

"Put your sword back in its place," Jesus said to him, "for all who draw the sword will die by the sword. Do you think I cannot call on my Father, and he will at once put at my disposal more than twelve legions of angels? But how then would the Scriptures be fulfilled that say it must happen in this way?"

Upon this approach Peter tried to protect his Lord with a sword but Jesus admonished him as if to accept this arrest which then left the disciples at a loss of what to do next.

As they led Jesus away, Simon Peter and John were the only ones to follow all the way to the high priest's courtyard to watch as Jesus was questioned. It was at this time while standing near the warmth of a fire that out of fear Simon Peter denied Jesus three times when asked if he was one of the disciples. His strength of mind had suddenly left as he became more aware of the situation around him much like when he was walking on water toward Jesus and became aware of the waves and began to sink. He had become afraid for his life.

Some of the disciples watched as there was a mock trial, brutal beating and crucifixion of their great teacher and leader. They had come to believe that this man was the "Anointed One of God" and now the Roman Empire that shouldn't have any power over a Messiah had taken him away from them. As Jesus hung on the cross which had become the most feared and most disgraceful way to die, we read that a few of the disciples and some of the important women in the life of Jesus had stood there in disbelief of the events unfolding before their very eyes.

It's hard to fully understand what was going through the minds of the disciples at this time for the writings are few, but we can see that they were confused and at a loss because everything lived in the past three years, which had become their way of life, was now unfolding. Not willing to go back to their old life, they simply gathered together within a locked room for comfort of brotherhood and fear of their lives.

What had just happened?

The few that were able to witness the death of Jesus on the cross shared these words.

Luke 23:46

> *Jesus called out with a loud voice, "Father, into your hands I commit my spirit." When he had said this, he breathed his last.*

They also recorded that after Jesus had died one of the centurions pierced his side with a sword to his heart making sure his death was complete.

The disciples had become convinced that everything about this Jesus was from God himself and that he had to be the Messiah yet now the chief priests, the very ones that were supposed to represent and teach of the Messiah, had used the Roman system to kill their hopes. Every comprehension from Jesus was now at question as we read that they gathered and conversed behind closed doors.

As the Sabbath was completed on the third day the women went to anoint the body of Jesus but we read upon arrival they found the stone sealing the tomb was removed and the body of Jesus was gone.

John 20:1, 2

> *Early on the first day of the week, while it was still dark, Mary Magdalene went to the tomb and saw that the stone had been removed from the entrance. So she came running to Simon Peter and the other disciple, the one Jesus loved, and said, "They have taken the Lord out of the tomb, and we don't know where they have put him!"*

When Simon Peter and the other disciple heard the news they quickly ran to the empty tomb to investigate but then returned to their homes in bewilderment.

John 20:10-18

> *Then the disciples went back to their homes, but Mary stood outside the tomb crying. As she wept, she bent over to look into the tomb and saw the two angels in white, seated where Jesus' body had been, one at the head and the other at the foot. They asked her, "Woman, why are you crying?"*

"They have taken my Lord away," she said, "and I don't know where they have put him." At this, she turned around and saw Jesus standing there, but she did not realize that it was Jesus.

"Woman," he said, "why are you crying? Who is it you are looking for?"

Thinking he was the gardener, she said, "Sir, if you have carried him away, tell me where you have put him, and I will get him."

Jesus said to her, "Mary."

She turned toward him and cried out in Aramaic, "Rabboni!" (which means Teacher). Jesus said, "Do not hold on to me, for I have not yet returned to the Father. Go instead to my brothers and tell them, 'I am returning to my Father and your Father, to my God and your God.'"

Mary Magdalene went to the disciples with the news: "I have seen the Lord!" And she told them that he had said these things to her.

The disciples were still trying to grasp the fact that their great teacher and Messiah hopes had just been crucified by the Romans, so what Mary Magdalene was telling them seemed like nonsense. But the writings tell us that it was not just Mary that had witnessed the living Jesus. In the book of Luke we read how Jesus walked up to a couple of men to converse with them as they were discussing the recent events of Israel and their dashed hopes.

Luke 24:17-21a

He asked them, "What are you discussing together as you walk along?"

They stood still, their faces downcast. One of them, named Cleopas, asked him, "Are you only a visitor to Jerusalem and do not know the things that have happened there in these days?"

"What things?" he asked.

"About Jesus of Nazareth," they replied. "He was a prophet, powerful in word and deed before God and all the people. The chief priests and our rulers handed him over to be sentenced to death, and they crucified him; but we had hoped that he was the one who was going to redeem Israel."

As they walked Jesus explained to them how the Christ had to suffer these things in order to come to his glory, but he went on to discuss all the Scriptures concerning himself to clarify within their minds the purpose of God. They had been amazed at the teachings of this traveler but it wasn't until they invited him to eat with them and the manner in which he gave thanks for the meal that they realized who it was that was dining with them.

Luke 24:30-35

> *When he was at the table with them, he took bread, gave thanks, broke it and began to give it to them. Then their eyes were opened and they recognized him, and he disappeared from their sight. They asked each other, "Were not our hearts burning within us while he talked with us on the road and opened the Scriptures to us?"*
>
> *They got up and returned at once to Jerusalem. There they found the Eleven and those with them, assembled together and saying, "It is true! The Lord has risen and has appeared to Simon." Then the two told what had happened on the way, and how Jesus was recognized by them when he broke the bread.*

With all the eyewitness accounts the disciples had not yet come to fully comprehend the whole situation. Jesus knew this group of men would need to be strong of heart and stand up against the tactics and pressures of Satan so he came to provide the proof their eyes and hearts would need to complete their full understanding and the mission they would now have to fulfill as they held the truth within their hearts.

John 20:19, 20

> *On the evening of that first day of the week, when the disciples were together, with the doors locked for fear of the Jews, Jesus came and stood among them and said, "Peace be with you!" After he said this, he showed them his hands and side. The disciples were overjoyed when they saw the Lord.*

After Jesus had proved to them that he was alive and his body was real he then taught Scriptures to them in order to reveal the complete and full picture of the purpose of the Christ.

Luke 24:46-49

> *He told them, "This is what is written: the Christ will suffer and rise from the dead on the third day, and repentance and forgiveness of sins will be preached in his name to all nations, beginning at Jerusalem. You are witnesses of these things. I am going to send you what my Father has promised; but stay in the city until you have been clothed with power from on high."*

Only then did the disciples realize that Christ Jesus died to pay for the sins of man so that all that believe will have eternal life with God. Only then did they realize the completeness of his mission. Only then did they grasp that God loves the whole world and wishes that none shall come to perish. With this absolute truth now captured within their hearts the disciples went on to set up churches, teach the love of God and become the witnesses God would use in sharing to the world the salvation offered through that sacrifice.

We expressed in chapter one the fact that we are still reading and teaching of Jesus over two thousand years later because the followers reported and documented that Jesus, who was proven dead, literally came back to life, exposed this fact to the disciples to prove he was given power and sent the disciples to teach the rest of the world.

Strength is given to their words because they could not withdraw, even when faced with death, from their teachings or writings. They had been given proof and witnessed with their own eyes and hands and it was God himself that revealed it. Because of this their fear and respect of God was stronger than their fear of a physical death.

The Apostle John was one of those who had witnessed it all and wrote these words to explain the entire reason of his gospel.

John 20:30, 31

> *Jesus did many other miraculous signs in the presence of his disciples, which are not recorded in this book. But these are written that you may believe that Jesus is the Christ, the Son of God, and that by believing you may have life in his name.*

The Apostle Paul further stated in strength the purpose of Christ in his letter to the Roman church.

Romans 3:21-25

> *But now a righteousness from God, apart from law, has been made known, to which the Law and the Prophets testify. This righteousness from God comes through faith in Jesus Christ to all who believe. There is no difference, for all have sinned and fall short of the glory of God, and are justified freely by his grace through the redemption that came by Christ Jesus. God presented him as a sacrifice of atonement, through faith in his blood.*

The purpose of the Christ had been completed and the hearts of the disciples had been directed. He therefore gave them one last commission.

Matthew 28:18-20

> *Then Jesus came to them and said, "All authority in heaven and on earth has been given to me. Therefore go and make disciples of all nations, baptizing them in the name of the Father and of the Son and of the Holy Spirit, and teaching them to obey everything I have commanded you. And surely I am with you always, to the very end of the age."*

Once the last command was given Jesus blessed them with his love and lifted before their very eyes.

Luke 24:50-52

> *When he had led them out to the vicinity of Bethany, he lifted up his hands and blessed them. While he was blessing them, he left them and was taken up into heaven. Then they worshiped him and returned to Jerusalem with great joy.*

When we have come to fully comprehend the completeness of this message then we understand the urgency of the message, so it therefore becomes our mission as well to go and make disciples throughout the world.

8

John 15

The writer of the Gospel of John was one of the actual disciples of Jesus, which thereby brings strength to the words in his accounts, as he was a witness to the miracles performed and teachings administered by Jesus.

The moments described in chapters thirteen through seventeen are the recollections of John on that final night of preparations and instructions from Jesus who knew the time had arrived for the Son to be glorified and return to the Father.

John 3:16, 17

> *For God so loved the world that he gave his one and only Son, that whoever believes in him shall not perish but have eternal life. For God did not send his Son into the world to condemn the world, but to save the world through him.*

If the message of the salvation offered was to be heard, the disciples would need the power of God to be able to teach, build churches and make disciples of all nations while at opposition to the lies and evils of Satan. Thus the message given within chapter fifteen is an acknowledgement of that power and thereby becomes one of the most important chapters of the New Testament that we need to hold within our heart.

First, in order to grasp a more complete comprehension of John chapter fifteen, we need to note a powerful message buried within a simple little story expressed in the book of Matthew.

In the time of Jesus it was common for uprisings to occur and false leaders to gather, so it is not surprising that one of the experts of the law would thereby come and test the teachings of Jesus.

Matthew 22:35-40

> *One of them, an expert in the law, tested him with this question: "Teacher, which is the greatest commandment in the Law?"*
>
> *Jesus replied: "'Love the Lord your God with all your heart and with all your soul and with all your mind.' This is the first and greatest commandment. And the second is like it: 'Love your neighbor as yourself.' All the Law and the Prophets hang on these two commandments."*

As we study the last night teachings of Jesus we clearly see that he warns the disciples to anticipate the complications of mankind throughout the world but expresses that life in God's hands is really this simple. All he asks of us is to love God and love others. So with this in mind let us begin our study of John chapter fifteen.

First, an overview of fifteen brings forth five key points. These points, if held within our hearts and minds, will sustain us in every aspect of the road we must travel and through all that God would have us endure.

Key Point One

Jesus is the true life-giving Vine.

In a vineyard the gardener removes the dead branches allowing the good branches the room and nutrients to produce more fruit. The gardener will also prune the branches that are producing fruit, causing them to branch out and produce even more fruit. With this understanding Jesus uses the vine as a metaphor to show the disciples the completeness of his very important message.

John 15:1, 2

> *I am the true vine, and my Father is the Gardener. He cuts off every branch in me that bears no fruit, while every branch that does bear fruit he prunes so that it will be even more fruitful.*

In the statement *"every branch in me"* Jesus explains that the branches represent those who have heard the message of Christ and profess to believe, for "in me" denotes being part of Jesus. But, just as the devil believes in Jesus and does not obey the teachings, so can people claim to know Jesus but not produce any fruit because he is not truly in their hearts. Thus, Jesus states that the Father removes and separates these non-producing branches from the vine to wither and become dead.

But if the believer is true in their commitment to Christ, much fruit will be produced. In other words, the one that comes to truly love Christ will follow his teachings and help many others to learn the love and salvation of God, but it is important to note that the representation of fruit in this passage also expresses the growth of the individual, as stated in Galatians 5:22, 23

> *But the fruit of the Spirit is love, joy, peace, patience, kindness, goodness, faithfulness, gentleness and self-control.*

Therefore the important distinction to be made of this metaphor is that, because he paid the penalty of sin, Jesus becomes the life-sustaining "Vine" that allows us access to the Father, while the Father as the gardener will remove all dead believers but nurture by way of teaching, testing, chiding and rewarding the fruit producing lives that grow from Christ.

Key Point two

Remain in Jesus

John 15:4, 5

> *Remain in me, and I will remain in you. No branch can bear fruit by itself; it must remain in the vine. Neither can you bear fruit unless you remain in me.*
>
> *I am the vine; you are the branches. If a man remains in me and I in him, he will bear much fruit; apart from me you can do nothing.*

We comprehend that a branch has to remain connected to the vine in order to live, but in the metaphor that Jesus uses with us as the branch and Jesus as the vine, if we don't stay connected with him does this mean we will die? Some would say "No", and yet others would say "Not in this life but in the life hereafter, for surely we do not stop breathing suddenly because we choose to live for ourselves." But this is not true, for when we choose to live for ourselves we have already died to the life that God had intended.

Previously we noted that God did not send his Son into the world to condemn the world, but to save the world through him which means that Jesus becomes the teachings, the living example and the life from God to us. So when Jesus told them to remain in him he was telling them to stay connected and live according to God's purpose. Therefore, if we profess to be one with Jesus, how then can we live for ourselves if to live for ourselves is to commit once again the original sin of Adam and Eve?

So then how do we remain in Jesus?

To remain in Jesus means to seek to know him, to trust in his direction, to reach out for his protection, to read about him, to pray through him, to praise him for his sacrifice, to worship him for he is God, to spend time with and meditate on his majesty. But to remain in Jesus also means to obey his teachings and his commands.

John 14: 23, 24a

> *Jesus replied, "If anyone loves me, he will obey my teaching. My Father will love him, and we will come to him and make our home with him. He who does not love me will not obey my teaching."*

Also in John 15:9, 10

> *As the father has loved me, so have I loved you. Now remain in my love. If you obey my commands, you will remain in my love, just as I have obeyed my Father's commands and remain in his love.*

With these passages Jesus clearly states that if we love him it will show in the life we live and the way we become as we grow from within. Our desire would naturally be to obey Jesus just as we would a loving father, for just as with a loving father we would have respect and wish to please him in all we do. As we travel afar, we would still conduct ourselves in a manner that is pleasing to our respected father for it is him that we represent even when we are away. As we stay connected to Jesus and our hearts grow to become more like him, we are also connected to the Heavenly Father because as Jesus clearly stated in John chapter ten verse thirty, he and the Father are one, thus by remaining in Jesus is to remain connected to the Father.

So what are the commands of Jesus?

John 15:12

> *My command is this: love each other as I have loved you.*

But remember, Satan would have us use our hearts to love ourselves rather than loving others thereby causing us to use free will to fulfill our own desires which is sin. So as Satan works the slow and painful separation of us from the Savior by providing the path to serve ourselves, we must, in order to combat this process, reach out to the word, teachings and guidance of Jesus in order to know the difference between the world's beliefs and those of God.

When we do not reach out to the teachings of Jesus then we become weak and allow Satan to be able to play us like a pawn on a chessboard. We become used and expendable as he furthers his destruction upon this earth at the expense of us and others that would come into our lives. The Gospel of Luke points out the warnings from Jesus as he spoke to a crowd expressing the snares of this earth if we do not follow his teachings.

Luke 6:49

> *But the one who hears my words and does not put them into practice is like a man who built a house on the ground without a foundation. The moment the torrent struck that house, it collapsed and its destruction was complete.*

These warnings show of the devastation that Satan can cause. Therefore we absolutely must submit ourselves fully to God.

James 4:7

> *Submit yourselves, then, to God. Resist the devil, and he will flee from you.*

This means that we need to watch over not only our actions but our thoughts and feelings as well. Paul understood just how important this was when he wrote his letter to the church of Corinth.

II Corinthians 10:5

> *We demolish arguments and every pretension that sets itself up against the knowledge of God, and we take captive every thought to make it obedient to Christ.*

But as stated in key point one if we profess to know Christ but continue to live for ourselves then we do not remain in Jesus and therefore do not produce any fruit. Jesus, as he teaches the disciples in his metaphor, clearly explains what would become of the believers that are not true of heart.

John 15:6

If anyone does not remain in me, he is like a branch that is thrown away and withers; such branches are picked up, thrown into the fire and burned.

Key Point Three

God's glory

John 15: 8

This is to my Father's glory, that you bear much fruit, showing yourselves to be my disciples.

A disciple is one who embraces and assists in spreading the teachings of another.

So what is it to be a disciple of Jesus?

Jesus had spent three years teaching his disciples to be of a different nature from that which was taught from the Pharisees, Sadducees and teachers of the Law. He had shown them by way of example to be caring, compassionate, kind, honest and forthright. He had taught them to serve one another as he had served them and he expressed that they even pray for those that spitefully use them.

As we study the ways of Jesus we note them as matters of the heart so to truly be a disciple of Christ is to allow our hearts to become Christ-like. As our hearts become true and are fully connected to Jesus how then can we retreat to only gather in churches or the comforts of our homes?

Matthew 5:14-16

You are the light of the world. A city on a hill cannot be hidden. Neither do people light a lamp and put it under a bowl. Instead they put it on its stand, and it gives light to everyone in the house. In the same way, let your light shine before men, that they may see your good deeds and praise your Father in heaven.

We must become true disciples of Jesus, for just as his disciples became Apostles, which is a messenger of God, it is important that we understand his new command to strengthen the resolve of the purpose of our hearts.

John 13:34, 35

A new command I give you: Love one another. As I have loved you, so you must love one another. By this all men will know that you are my disciples, if you love one another.

Therefore it is to the fullness of God and as a disciple of Jesus that we go and find the cold, the hungry, the heartbroken, the sick, the grief stricken, the lost and the abandoned and care for their needs. We need to love them back into the waiting arms of God. We need to teach them of hope for a future filled with the joy of Jesus. If we fall to the sin of selfishness we will find ourselves accepting the grace of God and then living for ourselves. When this happens we neglect the needs of the people within our lives.

Understand that a person does not wish to hear about the hope for a future when their immediate needs are with hunger, cold or of being sick. Therefore it becomes important that we meet these needs first and then their hearts and minds will listen to the message of the love of God. Jesus, wanting us to fully understand this concept, taught the following lesson of the completeness of love.

Matthew 25:42-45

"For I was hungry and you gave me nothing to eat, I was thirsty and you gave me nothing to drink, I was a stranger and you did not invite me in, I needed clothes and you did not clothe me, I was sick and in prison and you did not look after me."

They also will answer, "Lord, when did we see you hungry or thirsty or a stranger or needing clothes or sick or in prison, and did not help you?"

He will reply, "I tell you the truth, whatever you did not do for one of the least of these, you did not do for me."

When we reach out with the love of Christ truly in our hearts we then provide the path of God's people back to his loving arms which thereby becomes God's glory.

Key Point Four

We are not of this world

As we remain in Jesus our hearts grow to become more like the Father for, as Jesus clearly stated while conversing with the disciples, he and the Father are one.

John 14:9-10

Jesus answered: "Don't you know me, Philip, even after I have been among you such a long time? Anyone who has seen me has seen the Father. How can you say, 'Show us the Father'? Don't you believe that I am in the Father, and that the Father is in me? The words I say to you are not just my own. Rather, it is the Father, living in me, who is doing his work."

Therefore the strengths and understandings of Jesus are of a different comprehension for he was not made within the world but the world was made through him.

John 1:3

Through him all things were made; without him nothing was made that has been made.

We were born upon this world to physical laws whereas with Jesus the physical laws did not apply, which the disciples began to learn as they woke him in fear for their lives while caught in a storm as they crossed the lake.

Note: the disciples were mostly comprised of fishermen so for them to be afraid would mean that this was one powerful storm.

Luke 8:24, 25

The disciples went and woke him, saying, "Master, Master, we're going to drown!" He got up and rebuked the wind and the raging waters; the storm subsided, and all was calm. "Where is your faith?" he asked his disciples.

In fear and amazement they asked one another, "Who is this? He commands even the winds and the water, and they obey him."

Many times the disciples had witnessed with their own eyes how the physical laws did not apply to Jesus so as their minds began to accept to the point of mimic, we read an evidence of mere men performing the miraculous.

Matthew 14:28-31

> *"Lord, if it's you," Peter replied, "tell me to come to you on the water."*
>
> *"Come," He said.*
>
> *Then Peter got down out of the boat, walked on the water and came toward Jesus. But when he saw the wind, he was afraid and, beginning to sink, cried out, "Lord, save me!" Immediately Jesus reached out his hand and caught him. "You of little faith," he said, "why did you doubt?"*

We also see evidence of this in the Old Testament. Whenever and wherever God's purpose is being fulfilled man himself can be used by God to complete that purpose.

Exodus 14:21, 22

> *Then Moses stretched out his hand over the sea, and all that night the Lord drove the sea back with a strong east wind and turned it into dry land. The waters were divided, and the Israelites went through the sea on dry ground, with a wall of water on their right and on their left.*

But the important point being made in chapter fifteen is that as our hearts become more Christ-like then our lives become set apart from that of common beliefs of the world. God has therefore called us to a higher purpose and it thereby becomes our duty to avoid the ways of the world for it is filled with hatred, jealousy, malice, war and strife all encased with selfishness.

James 1:27

> *Religion that God our Father accepts as pure and faultless is this: to look after orphans and widows in their distress and to keep oneself from being polluted by the world.*

Jesus further warns us that the selfish desires of this earth will hate us because our life then courses against the grain of common belief.

John 15:18, 19

> *If the world hates you, keep in mind that it hated me first. If you belonged to the world, it would love you as its own. As it is, you do not belong to the world, but I have chosen you out of the world. That is why the world hates you.*

After all the teachings and final preparations, Jesus then looked toward heaven and prayed to the Father on behalf of the disciples.

John 17:14-16

> *I have given them your word and the world has hated them, for they are not of the world any more than I am of the world. My prayer is not that you take them out of the world but that you protect them from the evil one. They are not of the world, even as I am not of it.*

Key Point Five

We are not alone

Jesus knew that once he returned to the Father his disciples would have to stand against great opposition. First there were spiritual leaders of the Jews that had come to enjoy a great comfort, command and prestige and they would fight to uphold that position at all cost. Second, there was a complete Roman Empire that for the time being was only tolerating the Jewish community but had grown tired of their refusal to yield to the Roman beliefs. And third, Satan himself would do everything within his power to destroy any progress that God would take to reach out to his creation.

Understand Satan has no power against God but because man was given free will Satan knows he can work it to man's selfishness. But, if any man such as a disciple should stand strong to uphold and teach God's truth then Satan will work other weak minded men to oppose the strength of that individual.

God knew they would not be able to stand alone against such overwhelming odds. Therefore we read in John chapter fourteen as Jesus explains to the disciples that once he returned to the Father he would send them the Holy Spirit to help them in all endeavors.

John 14:15-18

> *If you love me, you will obey what I command. And I will ask the Father, and he will give you another Counselor to be with you forever - the Spirit of truth. The world cannot accept him, because it neither sees him nor knows him. But you know him, for he lives with you and will be in you. I will not leave you as orphans; I will come to you.*

So what is the Spirit of truth?

First of all, we know from the statement *"and will be in you"* that this Spirit will come to live within, but it is with further study that we learn of its purpose. According to scripture the Holy Spirit is here to teach, convict and guide through all oppositions.

John 14:26

> *But the Counselor, the Holy Spirit, whom the Father will send in my name, will teach you all things and will remind you of everything I have said to you.*

John 16:8

> *When he comes, he will convict the world of guilt in regard to sin and righteousness and judgment.*

John 16:13a

> *But when he, the Spirit of truth, comes, he will guide you into all truth.*

Thus, God did not leave them alone. With this power within comes the strength the disciples would need to stand strong against the comprehensions of the world, the selfishness of man and the works of Satan.

John 15:26

> *When the Counselor comes, whom I will send to you from the Father, the Spirit of truth who goes out from the Father, he will testify about me. And you also must testify, for you have been with me from the beginning.*

In the book of Acts we see a great example of this power as it becomes evident that Peter is not alone when he addresses a crowd, as the disciples, prompted by the Holy Spirit, reach out to accomplish the work of God.

Acts 2:22-24

> *Men of Israel , listen to this: Jesus of Nazareth was a man accredited by God to you by miracles, wonders and signs, which God did among you through him, as you yourselves know. This man was handed over to you by God's set purpose and foreknowledge; and you, with the help of wicked men, put him to death by nailing him to the cross. But God raised him from the dead, freeing him from the agony of death, because it was impossible for death to keep its hold on him.*

Acts 2:36-38

> *"Therefore let all Israel be assured of this: God has made this Jesus, whom you crucified, both Lord and Christ."*

> *When the people heard this, they were cut to the heart and said to Peter and the other apostles, "Brothers, what shall we do?"*

> *Peter replied, "Repent and be baptized, every one of you, in the name of Jesus Christ for the forgiveness of your sins. And you will receive the gift of the Holy Spirit. The promise is for you and your children and for all who are far off - for all whom the Lord our God will call."*

These were powerful words that convicted and taught the crowd, thereby showing the disciples were not alone to fend for themselves. As we now well know the Apostles were able to start and set the churches that taught of the loving grace of God as they became the teachers of the new covenant between God and all creation.

Furthermore the statement *"Repent and be baptized, every one of you, in the name of Jesus Christ for the forgiveness of your sins. And you will receive the gift of the Holy Spirit"* tells us that the Holy Spirit is for all that come to believe and therefore we too are not alone.

So the strength of Chapter fifteen clearly expresses that as we remain in Jesus, who is the connection between us and the Heavenly Father, and obey his commands, we will grow to become more like the Father and at the same time the work of God and the teachings of his love will be done through us by the Holy Spirit. Our responsibility therefore becomes that of choosing only to love God with all the innocence of a child.

Matthew 18:2-4

> *He called a little child and had him stand among them. And he said: "I tell you the truth, unless you change and become like little children, you will never enter the kingdom of heaven. Therefore, whoever humbles himself like this child is the greatest in the kingdom of heaven."*

This then brings us back to the message of the greatest commands expressed in the book of Matthew which is to love the Lord your God with all your heart and with all your soul and with all your mind, and love your neighbor as yourself.

All we have to do is Love and Love.

9

Stages of a Christian Walk

In previous chapters we discussed who God is, what he has done for us, how Satan has kept it from being obvious, whether or not if we as an individual are important to God, how to leave the sin behind and with innocence of heart how God's purpose is done through us. But now we need to discuss the stages toward completeness our hearts achieve as we walk in accordance with God.

So many Christians are brought to God with a story of saving grace and a promise of everlasting life. We hear the story and decide "that's for me." And then there are those of us who grew up in a Christian atmosphere and accept it because we know no other way. But the fact remains that most of us use this gift as some sort of insurance policy relying on God's grace, or the hope that it will be there when we die, while continuing to live for ourselves now.

It's hard to believe that we could accept this gift of love from God but then never allow the relationship to achieve any amount of progress. We call on him whenever we have trouble or need a parking space in front of a store and thank him whenever he answers our prayers but forget to spend time with him when our lives are doing just fine.

When we accept God in this fashion we are robbing ourselves of the greatest relationship we will ever have. So in this final chapter it is with the hope of achieving a more complete relationship with God that we discuss the stages our hearts and minds will naturally take in an obedient and proper walk with our Creator.

First Stage

Acceptance and Commitment

When someone comes into our life to tell us the story of the saving grace of Jesus we then have two options of response. We can walk away shaking our heads in disbelief rejecting it, or we can accept and believe. If we should come to believe then a commitment to God is made.

But it is only to the level of availability within each individual that we accept the word. Jesus, in his parable of four different soils, explains the amount of commitment that each will take in accordance to their understandings.

Mark 4:3-8

> *Listen! A farmer went out to sow his seed. As he was scattering the seed, some fell along the path, and the birds came and ate it up. Some fell on rocky places, where it did not have much soil. It sprang up quickly, because the soil was shallow. But when the sun came up, the plants were scorched, and they withered because they had no root. Other seed fell among thorns, which grew up and choked the plants, so that they did not bear grain. Still other seed fell on good soil. It came up, grew and produced a crop, multiplying thirty, sixty, or even a hundred times.*

Because the disciples were unable to fully comprehend the parable, Jesus then took the time to explain it.

Mark 4:14-20

> *The farmer sows the word. Some people are like seed along the path, where the word is sown. As soon as they hear it, Satan comes and takes away the word that was sown in them. Others, like seed sown on rocky places, hear the word and at once receive it with joy. But since they have no root, they last only a short time. When trouble or persecution comes because of the word, they quickly fall away. Still others, like seed sown among thorns, hear the word; but the worries of this life, the deceitfulness of wealth and the desires for other things come in and choke the word, making it unfruitful. Others, like seed sown on good*

soil, hear the word, accept it, and produce a crop-thirty, sixty or even a hundred times what was sown.

With this explanation the disciples were able to understand just how limited the levels of acceptance and commitment of an individual would be. We too, when we compare this parable to our lives, can see, if any, the limits in the dedication of our own personal commitment, and depending upon the moments of our life we will find that this parable can also represent the levels of commitment at any given time. Sometimes we will be drawn in by the desires of this earth and other times we will be fully committed to the servitude of Christ.

Second Stage

Obedience

This is the stage that will tell of our level of commitment, for if the commitment is superficial then this stage will trip us up.

The majority of Christians can't get past this stage. They will spend their whole life fluctuating between the first and this second stage. Because of convictions of the heart they will repent for sins committed but then fall back to selfish desires when temptation resurfaces.

Understand that if we as Christians give only of ourselves according to our availability then we are in trouble, for most of us are not ready to relinquish the full control of our lives. We may feel we believe in God but to let someone else have complete control of our destination is hard for us to do, and it tests the very boundaries of the foundation of our belief.

In our defense, we were born and live in a world that teaches us to "grab the bull by the horns" and take charge of our lives, but as we have learned in John chapter fifteen we are no longer of this world and should let God have full control as he would be able to care for us far better than we could ever care for ourselves.

But here it is: Stage Two, which calls for us to be obedient to Christ. But why should this trip us up? For have we not already learned that to be obedient to Christ is to love God with all your heart, mind and soul, and love others as yourself? So with these two commandments fully empowered within our hearts it would therefore be easy for us to be obedient. The only reason we are not fully obedient is that free will affords us the ability to be selfish and care for our own needs before others. Remember the passage mentioned just a few paragraphs ago that stated *"but the worries of this life, the deceitfulness of wealth and the desires for other things come in and choke the word, making it unfruitful."* Therefore we must deny ourselves to become more obedient to God.

Luke 9:23, 24

> *Then he said to them all: "If anyone would come after me, he must deny himself and take up his cross daily and follow me. For whoever wants to save his life will lose it, but whoever loses his life for me will save it."*

In this passage Jesus is not asking us to give up our lives in the physical sense but to commit fully to God our lives which he gave to us in the first place so that he may use them to bring others to know his salvation. He is asking us to deny any personal gratifications in order to care for others that are without the love of God. And he promises that any denial of self now will be rewarded later in heaven.

But when we are committed to saving our lives or to building them according to personal goals and plans then we will spend the rest of our days going from commitment to disobedience to repentance and back to commitment once again; never growing, never enjoying, never fully living the glorious life that God so graciously longs to provide for us. We only cheat ourselves.

Third Stage
Submission

When we as Christians learn to suppress the tendencies of selfish desires and remain obedient to Christ then we will allow ourselves to reach this third stage of submission. In this stage we will find that as we are more in touch with the path that God sets or the door that God opens we become more content with the direction of our life. We learn that life under the guidance of God brings more gratification, comfort and fulfillment than anything we could muster alone.

The Christian that finally reaches this stage will suddenly realize an incredible freedom that comes with submission. We have no worries, no plans, no goals and no reason to be upset.

Example: If we have not come to be submissive and should see a particular job that we believe meets the prestige we feel we deserve and the money that will better acquire the things we crave, then if the door should be closed by God for whatever reason, we will find ourselves upset, and possibly blame God himself for not giving it to us, disallowing the knowledge that God would have of the future and the direction he set to better care for our needs. But if our hearts have reached the level of submission then we will be content to know that whatever happens is to the glory of God.

The Apostle Paul went on to build churches to the opposition of great evil and was eventually thrown into prison for it. With the love of God embedded fully within his heart he was dedicated to saving every soul possible for he understood the deceitful ways of Satan and the loving grace of God.

Luke 15:10

In the same way, I tell you, there is rejoicing in the presence of the angels of God over one sinner who repents.

Paul frequented these churches throughout Europe to ensure their progress but was unable to attend once he was put in prison. Being submissive to God he did not question his motive but turned to the privileges afforded him as a Roman citizen. Paul was just concerned with one soul at a time and continued his work accordingly but as each Roman guard and each prisoner was converted to the love of Christ and went out to teach others it shook the very foundations of the Roman Empire.

Paul understood that all things work to the glory of God and therefore kept steady to his work regardless of being in prison. He knew that God was fully in charge so he then kept in touch with the churches by way of messages but had no idea of the repercussions of those letters we are reading two thousand plus years later that comprise a good portion of the New Testament. God's purpose was being fulfilled but Paul had no comprehension of the amount of work God was doing through him. He was just being submissive.

Fourth Stage

Joy

When we are obedient to God our hearts grow to be one with him. As our hearts become filled to overflowing with the love of the Father, which comes to live within us, then our lives, hearts, minds and attitudes become filled with the joy of Jesus.

John 15:9-11

> As the Father has loved me, so have I loved you. Now remain in my love. If you obey my commands, you will remain in my love, just as I have obeyed my Father's commands and remain in his love. I have told you this so that my joy may be in you and that your joy may be complete.

Understand that once we sin the joy goes from us for God did not make our hearts to enjoy sin. Remember sin brings a degradation of the heart causing a sadness of spirit, so only when we repent does the soul rejoice. Therefore if we should slip and fall from grace, we must crawl back into God's waiting arms with a contrite heart and repent for our sins so that we may have complete joy once again.

When we have real joy then our lives become more fulfilled even at opposition from the world and the evils that Satan weaves within the moral fabric of society. We will play amongst the dangers like children with innocent minds and playful hearts while under the protection of God Almighty.

Fifth Stage
Servitude

As our lives become more proper to the comprehension and completion of God and the way we were intended to be, then our hearts become filled with a true love, a Godly love, instead of self-love, therefore we long to care for one another to make sure of each other's needs. When this happens we naturally have desire to serve others for we truly love them.

Jesus performed an example of this when he washed the feet of the disciples, which was the work of a menial servant in the eyes of the world, in order to help them understand the heart of anyone that would call themselves a disciple of Christ.

Jesus mentioned many times throughout his ministry that those who serve will be first in the kingdom of heaven because they have the love of God within them, for Jesus himself served to the completeness of his death to pay for the sins of the world.

Mark 10:42-45

> *Jesus called them together and said, "You know that those who are regarded as rulers of the Gentiles lord it over them, and their high officials exercise authority over them. Not so with you. Instead, whoever wants to become great among you must be your servant, and whoever wants to be first must be slave of all. For even the Son of Man did not come to be served, but to serve, and to give his life as a ransom for many."*

Jesus further tells us that we are to become complete like children and only then will we be of the proper heart of God.

Matthew 18:3, 4

> *And he said: "I tell you the truth, unless you change and become like little children, you will never enter the kingdom of heaven. Therefore whoever humbles himself like this child is the greatest in the kingdom of heaven."*

It is therefore a matter of the heart, for to truly be like God is to love with such completeness, humbleness and innocence that we put others before ourselves, which is to serve them in such a way that they too may know God.

Sixth Stage

Sons and Daughters of God

This is it. This is the destination that God longs for all his creation to reach. Through the sacrifice of Jesus we are given the ability to become sons and daughters of the Almighty God.

John 1:12

> *Yet to all who received him, to those who believed in his name, he gave the right to become children of God.*

When he created us it was with the purpose to enjoy and cherish us but we sinned when we disobeyed God, which brought a separation from the Father. He created us and then we walked away from him, which broke his heart for he dearly loved us.

How dearly?

We are given a great example in the book of Luke as we read of Jesus telling of parables and the importance of each individual because the Pharisees and teachers of the Law had become indignant toward Jesus for spending time with people that they had deemed beneath their standards. The third parable is the story of a father and two sons of which the younger set out in his own direction seeking for himself. This parable has become known as the "Prodigal Son".

Luke 15:11-24

> *Jesus continued: "There was a man who had two sons. The younger one said to his father, 'Father, give me my share of the estate.' So he divided his property between them.*
>
> *"Not long after that, the younger son got together all he had, set off for a distant country and there squandered his wealth in wild living. After he had spent everything, there was a severe famine in that whole country, and he began to be in need. So he went and hired himself out to a citizen of that country, who sent him to his fields to feed pigs. He longed to fill his stomach with the pods that the pigs were eating, but no one gave him anything.*
>
> *When he came to his senses, he said, 'How many of my father's hired men have food to spare, and here I am starving to death! I will set out and go back to my father and say to him: Father, I have sinned against heaven and against you. I am no longer worthy to be called your son; make me like one of your hired men.'*
>
> *So he got up and went to his father.*
>
> *But while he was still a long way off, his father saw him and was filled with compassion for him; he ran to his son, threw his arms around him and kissed him.*
>
> *The son said to him, 'Father, I have sinned against heaven and against you. I am no longer worthy to be called your son.'*
>
> *But the father said to his servants, 'Quick! Bring the best robe and put it on him. Put a ring on his finger and sandals on his feet. Bring the fattened calf and kill it. Let's have a feast and celebrate. For this son of mine was dead and is alive again; he was lost and is found' So they began to celebrate."*

This younger son had sinned greatly against all that was proper and had definitely shamed the family name. He had obviously rid himself of the family ring and now had bare feet as was the custom of a slave. He knew that the sin was his and could blame no one but himself. When he had come to his senses realizing that his father's servants were in a better position than himself, he then, with contrite heart, was hoping that he could be hired by his father as a servant.

He had come to know that what he did was shameful and had hoped that his father would at least hear his plea for a job for he knew he deserved nothing more. *"Father, I have sinned against heaven and against you. I am no longer worthy to be called your son; make me like one of your hired men."*

This is the heart of someone that has truly learned that he had made a great error in judgment and had shamed all that his father stood for. He was greatly sorry for his actions and hoped for a new start but he truly believed that he should only be given a job as a hired servant.

But the parable tells us that as he was still far off his father recognized and ran to him. This means that the father was waiting, watching and longing for his son that had left him. It further states that the father's actions were not that of an angry man who had lost a great amount of money because of the son, or that he expressed anger for the wrong he committed against the family name, but that he was more concerned for the return of a dear loved one that has come back to the father and the place where he belonged.

In this parable when the son could no longer see himself as such the father confirmed him as son and rejoiced for he was back within his loving care. This parable tells of the love of a father for his lost son. It tells of the father's concern that his son's shame is covered, the family crest be replaced on his finger and that sandals be placed back on his feet. It tells of the fact that even though the son knew he deserved nothing the father had such a great love for the lost son that he threw a feast to celebrate his return. *"For this son of mine was dead and is alive again; he was lost and is found."*

This is the love that God has for his creation. He longs for all to return to him and he longs for all to reach an understanding that we are his sons and daughters.

This is the Ultimate Goal of God: that we come back to his waiting loving arms as sons and daughters.

Romans 8:16, 17

> *The Spirit himself testifies with our spirit that we are God's children. Now if we are children, then we are heirs - heirs of God and co-heirs with Christ, if indeed we share in his sufferings in order that we may also share in his glory.*

Notes

All Bible quotes within this book are from the NIV except where noted.